The Sensory Detective Curriculum

Discovering Sensory Processing and How It Supports Attention, Focus & Regulation Skills

Meets learning goals in science & social studies!

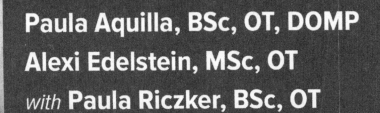

Paula Aquilla, BSc, OT, DOMP

Alexi Edelstein, MSc, OT

with **Paula Riczker, BSc, OT**

The Sensory Detective Curriculum

All marketing and publishing rights guaranteed to and reserved by:

721 W. Abram St. Arlington, TX 76013

Phone: 817.277.0727

Toll free: 800.489.0727

Fax: 817.277.2270

Online: www.sensoryworld.com

Email: info@sensoryworld.com

ISBN: 9781935567608

Dedication

The Sensory Detective Curriculum is dedicated to all the courageous students who try so hard to be successful everyday and the dedicated teachers who support them.

Acknowledgements

Thank you to my best friend and husband, Mark, for his love, humor, support, and generosity. Thank you to my wonderful daughters Katie and Ella, who shared their wonderful ideas and editing talents. I'd like to thank my parents, Ray and Dorothy. Thank you to Jennifer, Leta, and the team at Sensory World for believing in this curriculum and for helping to make it a reality. Thank you to all the wonderful children, families, and educators I have been privileged to meet, support, and learn from. It does take a village to raise a child, and the school is that village—that very important village that helps prepare children for life!

— *Paula*

Thank you to my wonderful husband, Mark, for his never ending support and believing in me. To my parents, Susie and Eitan, thank you for always encouraging me and leading by example. Thank you to all the families with whom I have worked who taught me so much over the years. Thank you to all the wonderful people I worked alongside who have shared their amazing ideas with me, including all the professionals, teachers, and school staff. To Paula Aquilla, thank you so much for your incredible mentorship. Finally and most importantly, I dedicate my work here to my sister, Michelle. Even though you are faced with many challenges, you have by far taught me the most!

— *Alexi*

Thank you to my husband, Allon, for always being exceptionally supportive and encouraging of everything I do. To Aubrey, Leah and Aviva—thank you for teaching me something new every day and for always bringing spirit, fun, and laughter to the table. Many thanks to Paula Aquilla for her support, guidance, and for helping me become a better clinician. Thank you to all the amazing families and children I have the pleasure of working with. This book is written for you to inspire others to learn and understand how we can all be our best selves.

— *Paula R.*

Contents

Introduction

Who Are We and Why Did We Write This Curriculum?

We are a group of occupational therapists, who work in clinical, home, and school settings. We take every opportunity to share information to empower children, families, and teachers. We are often called into school meetings to problem solve around challenging behaviors. Sharing information about the reasons why behaviors occur in the first place is the most effective way to solve problems. We often find that the solutions are easy once you understand what is happening.

We decided to write a curriculum that could be used in a school setting to educate children, teachers, and parents about sensory processing so this information can be shared.

The Toronto District School Board highlights a positive character trait for children to learn about each month. We often wondered, "How do children learn about character traits when they may not even know how to interpret the signals from their own nervous system and body? How do we get from understanding the way we work to understanding the character traits we want to develop in ourselves?" The idea of *The Sensory Detective Curriculum* was born! We met weekly for a year to put this curriculum together. It has undergone many changes and updates. Several of our OT colleagues, teacher colleagues, and parents have read and helped us to shape this curriculum—thanks to all of you for your time and advice.

What Is a Sensory Detective Curriculum?

This curriculum is a guide to teach children in grades 1 to 4 about their nervous system and sensory processing with the goal of helping them understand the way they work. There are many hands-on activities to enable their learning to come to life! This curriculum is also a journey of self-exploration. Children will learn about their own nervous system and sensory preferences, and discover that the sensory preferences of their friends may be different. They will gain an understanding and appreciation of the differences in how people function.

How Is the Sensory Detective Curriculum Used?

The Sensory Detective Curriculum is divided into seven chapters, each with learning objectives and hands-on activities. Chapter 4 puts all the learning about sensory processing into practice. It is a lot of FUN! Chapters 5 and 6 outline other amazing ways to enable children to better understand their nervous system and learn about self-regulation. Chapter 7 introduces the characteristics that children can learn in school and offers activities to deepen their own character development.

The Sensory Detective Curriculum can augment the science curriculum and the social studies curriculum, and can easily be incorporated into a classroom setting and home setting.

Who Can Benefit from Reading This Curriculum?

We can all benefit from knowing ourselves better. Teachers, school administrators, parents, therapists, and children can benefit from reading this curriculum. The better we understand ourselves, the better we can maintain our own calm, alert states. The better we understand others, the better we can tolerate differences and support and even celebrate our diversity. The better we understand each other, the better we move forward as a group, a school, and a society.

Hidden gems that can be learned in this curriculum:

- everyone develops at their own speed; we're all on the same road
- the best learning and our very best selves happen when we are calm and alert and sensory strategies can help maintain our calm, alert state
- acceptance and inclusion increase when we understand ourselves and one another
- increased understanding of our similarities and difference equals less fear of our differences
- we move forward as a group when we take responsibility for each other and this is how we build a strong, caring and kind society
- knowing ourselves enables us to make better decisions about our behavior, our choices, and our future
- children learn by example; let's set a good one!
- quality of life increases when our environment matches our nervous system

Tips to enhance learning:

- be creative; this curriculum is a guide and feel free to add any activities you feel will help your students/children learn the objectives
- incorporate as many learning opportunities as possible; carry over examples from the classroom, the community and current events
- involve parents—when learning generalizes to home it can be better understood and learned
- acknowledge the efforts and successes of people—it helps increase the motivation to learn!
- have fun!

Conclusion

The Sensory Detective Curriculum has been a real labor of love. We have combined our learning, creativity, time, and experiences to put it together for you. It is our hope that you find it helpful and that your students/children learn about themselves and each other. It is our hope that positive changes happen in your students/children in your classrooms, in your schools, and in your communities. Big positive changes happen when you add up all the small positive changes! It is our hope that you enjoy your learning, build the school culture that you dream of, and have a lot of fun! Be kind to each other!

— *Paula Aquilla, Alexi Edelstein & Paula Riczker*

Chapter One

Sensory Processing and Sensations

Learning Objectives—
In this chapter, teachers and students will learn:

- Definitions of sensory processing, sensory integration, and sensory regulation
- Development of sensory integration
- Development of sensory regulation
- Body sensations—proprioception, tactile, vestibular, and interoception
- Environment sensations—vision, auditory, olfactory, and gustatory
- Where sensory processing happens
- Research
- Sensory Processing as a foundation for function
- Sensory Processing Disorders
- The stages of sensory processing

Help Me Understand Sensory Processing—What Is It?

You put your hand in your desk to get your pencil case. Your hand feels around until you touch a large, flexible, soft bag with a bumpy zipper on top! Your hand grasps your pencil case and you pull it out of your desk. You have successfully used your tactile (touch) system to identify and retrieve the object you were looking for!

We have many senses that provide our brain with information about our bodies and environment and we put all this sensory information together to understand what is happening in our bodies and environment. This is called sensory processing. We take in, sort, and organize a sensation so that we can attach meaning to it. The whole process of organizing the sensation and attaching meaning to it is called sensory integration. Once interpreted, the sensory information guides the motor response and we can respond to the sensation with an action.

The Development of Sensory Integration

Our brain is beautifully designed and always processing information from our body and the environment—even when we are asleep! We have many senses that give us important information about ourselves and the world around us. Some of the senses develop early and give us information when we are tiny babies, still growing in our mom! The senses that develop first involve the vestibular system, which gives us information about movement, our auditory (hearing) system, and our tactile system. These sensory systems are firing before we are even born! Moms report that babies often move in response to certain voices in their mom's environment or to music. They also respond to their mom's movement and can calm down when the mom walks or rocks in a rocking chair. The unborn baby can also interpret touch and calm down when the mom rubs her tummy. Isn't that amazing?

Sensory integration continues to develop throughout our lifetime. Every activity or environment offers opportunities to practice how to process sensation.

Sensory Regulation

Unborn babies can calm themselves by moving around inside their mom or pushing against their mom's body. Some babies can calm themselves by sucking their thumb. The ability to use sensation to calm and regulate our body begins even before we are born. Regulation through sensation is an amazing process that we use early in our development and throughout our life.

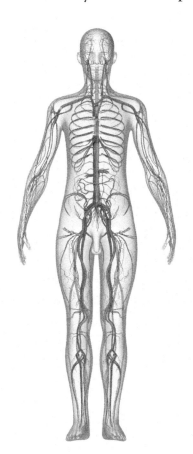

Understanding the way our nervous system works and processes sensation can help us understand ourselves better. When we understand ourselves better, we can become aware of what sensation our nervous system needs so that we can maintain a calm, alert state. This ability is called regulation. Regulation is a life skill that is necessary for success in school, social settings, self-care, and work. We all benefit from knowing how to use sensation to keep our nervous systems calm and alert.

The emotional part of our brain (the limbic system) is a neighbor to the brainstem (the sensory processing part of our nervous system) and each system can affect the other. Regulated sensory processing helps us feel calm. When we feel calm, we can better process sensory information.

The limbic system has many pathways that connect it to different parts of the brain. The frontal lobe, located behind the forehead, has many pathways connecting it to the limbic system. The frontal lobe is responsible for our executive functions, which we will learn about in Chapters 5 and 6. Our ability to solve problems, control our impulses, and sequence our motor responses represents executive functions. Executive functions help us manage our behavior. Our sensory processing, emotions, and behavior are all connected. Regulation of our sensory processing can help us regulate our emotions and behavior.

Teachers and parents play a critical role in encouraging the development of self-regulation, that is, sensory, emotional, and behavioral regulation in children. A teacher may use several strategies to manage behavior in the classroom setting; however, if we all learn how to regulate our own sensory processing and our own emotions, our behavior can be regulated as a consequence.

Focusing on maintaining the nervous system in a calm, alert state through efficient sensory processing can enable all of us to better manage our emotions and behavior.

The intent of this curriculum is for teachers and students to learn about sensory processing so that they can use the strategies to stay regulated in the classroom setting. We will learn about the neurology of sensory processing, sensory processing disorders, and assessment. Also, a self-discovery chapter is full of fun activities! Sensory strategies are called bottom-up strategies because they work from the physical body. Chapters 5 through 7 will discuss top-down strategies, the strategies that use language and cognition. Both bottom-up and top-down strategies are necessary for a classroom that strives to support regulation.

When we speak about sensory processing, we must understand that we process many different sensations at the same time. No senses act in isolation; however, to understand the different senses, we will dissect the senses and look at each one individually. Then we'll put them back together to look at the system as a whole.

Sensory Integration

Sensory integration, which is sometimes called sensory processing, is the process of putting together and interpreting sensory information we receive from our body and from the environment. Efficient sensory integration contributes to efficient perception, learning, accurate movement and social interaction.

Our ability to attend to and focus on something means that we can process some sensation automatically and focus on the sensation that we need to perform a particular task. For example, during a spelling test, students focus on and attend to the teacher's voice and ignore the sounds of papers rustling and voices from the hallway. They focus on the visual information that comes from their printing and ignore the other marks on the desk and the colorful posters on the wall. Efficient sensory processing enables this ability to focus on some sensory input while screening out sensation that is not important to the task at hand. If we couldn't do this sensory screening, we would constantly be bombarded with sensation and become exhausted!

Body Sensation—Proprioception

Let's get acquainted with sensory processing by first learning about senses that bring us information about our own body. We use this information to determine where we are in relation to our environment.

Close your eyes and describe your body's position.
- Are you standing/sitting or lying down?
- Are your legs crossed?
- Are your hands in your pockets?

The information we receive about our body's position is provided through our *proprioception* system. The proprioception system has two duties. It is the sensory system that gives our brain information about the position of our body and it enables us to know how much pressure to put through our pencil or how to hug with just the right amount of pressure!

Our proprioception system also helps us determine whether we are comfortable. If you are wearing rain boots that are too small, your proprioception receptors in your feet are screaming "OUCH! We are squished and have no room to move!" Your feet may be uncomfortable because you need a larger pair of boots!

We use our proprioception system all the time. It allows us to maintain our posture and position ourselves in relation to others and objects in our environment. It also helps us judge the pressure of the force we use in our tasks. For example, it helps us push a door open with enough pressure to open it but not enough pressure to bang it against the wall.

Tactile Sensation

Our touch system, which is called our *tactile* system, provides information about things that we touch and things that are touching us, like a T-shirt. It also gives us information about what is inside our mouths, like our toothbrush or the sandwich we are eating for lunch. Our tactile system enables us to feel wind on our skin and our hair moving in the wind. We use our tactile system all the time. Most of the touch, like the touch of our socks, underwear, and the rest of our clothing, can be ignored throughout the day; we are processing the touch our clothing provides but we don't need to focus on it unless it is new or uncomfortable. The touch of our chair under us, the feeling of our shoes, and feeling our hair against our ear can all be ignored as we choose to focus on the touch of the pencil in our hand so that we can move it correctly to make, for example, the letter K.

Vestibular Sensation

Our balance system is called our *vestibular* system. It provides us with information about our position in relation to earth's gravity. This system tells us if we are moving or still, how fast we are moving, and the direction in which we are moving. This system is extremely important; it gives us information all the time so that we don't fall! The vestibular system is called the master sense because it provides extra information to help our vision and auditory systems make more sense. It helps keep our head straight so that we can use our eyes and ears accurately and efficiently. The vestibular system also works with the proprioception system to help us maintain our posture against gravity. When information from our vestibular system is processed well, it helps us better process information from our other senses.

Interoception Sensation

Information from our internal body and the smooth muscles of our organs is carried through the *interoception* system. This system tells us when we have to go to the washroom and when we are hungry. It is the sensory system that provides our brain with information from the inside of our body. It tells us if we are tense because we are excited for recess, if our tummy is in a knot because we have a math test, and if we are relaxed after we have added yoga to our daily physical activity.

Environment Sensation—Vision

We also have sensory systems that provide us with information about our environment. These systems bring information to our brains about what is happening in our classroom, in the playground, and on the bus.

The vision system carries information about what we see in our environment. We use this system to look at things that are far away, like a bird flying across the sky, and things that are close, like the book we are reading. Part of our vision system is used to focus on and look at the details of items and part of the vision system is used for balance.

Auditory Sensation

We listen with our *auditory* system, which gives us information about the sounds in our environment. We hear specific sounds, like the sound of the teacher's voice asking you to take out your math book, and general sounds, like the sounds from the playground at recess.

Olfactory Sensation

Information about smells enters our brain through the *olfactory* system in our nose. This system is highly sensitive and can make our brain pay attention to a new smell, especially if the smell is a bad one!

Gustatory Sensation

The *gustatory* system gives our brain information about what we taste. Sometimes things taste right in our mouth, like the yummy pizza on pizza day. We can also sometimes taste smells that are in the air, like the salt in the winter air when street crews have salted the icy roads.

Our brain can put all this information together to give us information in three dimensions! Sensory integration enables us to know what is happening in our bodies and what is happening in our environment in real time. It's absolutely marvelous!

Putting All the Senses Together

When we go outside for recess, we feel our clothing as we move toward the playground. We keep our balance on the stairs and we know the position of our body, which enables us to turn corners and make it through the doorway. Once we are outside, we scan the playground using our vision and auditory systems to find our friends who are organizing a game of baseball. We switch from walking to running. We don't fall because our vestibular and proprioception systems are working together to give us a constant flow of the information we need to stay upright. We may bite into our crunchy apple and taste that yummy goodness at the same time! We find our friends and begin to play.

When all the senses work together to give us information about our body and environment, and we interpret this information, it is called sensory integration. The process of streamlining that information, because there is a lot of information, is called sensory processing.

Where Does Sensory Processing Happen?

Sensory processing happens in a part of our central nervous system called the brain stem. The brain stem is like a relay station; all the information enters here and is filtered here. Important information comes into our focus and unimportant information is discarded. The brain stem works with another system called the limbic (emotional) system, to determine what is important and what can be ignored in that moment. For example, when we go down the stairs, information from our vestibular, proprioceptive, tactile, and visual systems comes into focus to ensure that we don't fall. We don't pay as much attention to our olfactory or gustatory systems in this task. However, on pizza day, when we eat a delicious slice of hot cheesy pizza, our brain pays more attention to our olfactory and gustatory systems so that we can enjoy the taste of the pizza.

Once the brain stem has filtered the sensory information, if the limbic system determines that it is important, it is relayed up to the brain and interpreted so that we can choose a motor response or reply. When our friend calls our name, our auditory system takes the information in, combines it with visual, vestibular, proprioceptive, and tactile information, and sends it up to our brain. We can interpret that our name has been called, who called it, what was said, and where we are in relation to our friend so that we can reply.

Sensory processing is an amazing ability of our nervous system to give us the information we need to take care of ourselves and participate in our environment.

Information from the senses is like the ingredients we use when we make a cake. We need all the ingredients for our cake to turn out and be delicious. If we are missing even one ingredient, our cake may not turn out.

When we catch a ball, our "ingredients" are the information we receive from:

- Our vestibular system—keeps us upright
- Our proprioception system—tells us about the position of our body
- Our visual system—tells us where the ball is in relation to us
- Our tactile system—tells us when the ball touches our hand

We put all these sensory ingredients together, interpret them, and voila! We catch the ball!

Dr. Jean Ayres—OT with a Vision

Dr. Jean Ayres (Figure 1.1) was an amazing occupational therapist (OT) who performed pioneering work in the area of sensory integration. She worked with children and wanted to know more about how their nervous system organized and interpreted sensory information. Dr. Ayres described sensory processing disorder as a "traffic jam" in the brain. She studied and used her treatment techniques on many children and the children learned how to improve the organization and interpretation of information from their senses. Her treatment techniques were also fun! She used swings, bouncy balls, pools of sand and rice,

Figure 1.1

Dr. Jean Ayres (photo courtesy of her family)

trampolines, scooters, and many other fun activities. The children had fun playing and learning at the same time!

Research in Sensory Processing

Many people from many disciplines have become interested in sensory processing and continued the research of Dr. Ayres. The following studies are a sample of the expanding body of research in sensory processing:

The prevalence of sensory processing disorder—sensory over-responsiveness (SPD-SOR) was found to be 16% in a study of 7- to 10-year-olds (Ben Sasson et al., 2009). Teresa May-Benson et al. (2009) explored risk factors and identified low birth weight, pre-natal complications, maternal stress, illness, and birth complications. Goldsmith et al. (2006) reported possible genetic susceptibility for tactile and auditory sensory over-responsiveness.

Internalizing problems like anxiety and externalizing problems like aggression are other challenges that an individual with SPD may face (Ben-Sasson et al., 2009). Another study cited decreases in daily life activities in those with SPD (Bar-Shalita et al., 2008).

Adults with SPD can experience social and emotional difficulties and impairments in quality of life, including anxiety, decreased general health, and increased body pain (Kinnealey et al., 2011).

Other researchers have investigated physiological differences in people with SPD versus other conditions, including treatment for SPD (Miller et al., 2007). The effects of SPD on a family include parental stress, exhaustion, and isolation (Carter et al., 2011), as well as decreased feelings of parental competence (Cohen et al., 2011). Research on the characteristics of disorders that are comorbid with SPD are discussed in Chapters 5 and 6.

Teachers and students, we want to share information about sensory processing with you so that you can understand your own nervous system better and learn activities that will help you stay calm and happy in the classroom. We can see our behaviors from many perspectives. The perspective of sensory processing enables us to understand the behaviors we use for self-regulation. We can then use sensory activities to help us stay calm and alert so that we can learn and have fun in the classroom.

Sensory Processing As the Foundation

Sensory processing is like the foundation of a building (see Figure 1.2). When the foundation is strong, it can support many skills built on it.

As we process information from our vestibular and proprioception systems, we develop muscle tone and begin our relationship with gravity. This relationship continues throughout our lifetime. We develop posture and stay upright against the pull of gravity. Accurate processing of vestibular information enables us to develop balance skills to transfer our weight and become comfortable changing positions and moving in space. We need to know the pull of gravity to achieve balance. Eye movements that are necessary to follow the lines of words in a book or the teacher's writing on the board also depend on our vestibular system.

As tiny infants, we use our tactile and proprioception systems to eat. We begin to suck to drink and learn that it feels good to eat. We struggle to move against gravity and it feels good to gain control over our movements. We want the toy across the room and it feels good to see it, move toward it, and get it! Sensory processing enables many connections in our development. We see things and move toward them. We put something in our mouth and enjoy the texture and taste. We hug our mom and dad and enjoy the warmth and love of their responding hug. The emotions that we experience from our early sensory experiences motivate us to repeat the actions, practice the sensory processing, and experience the emotions over and over again, laying the blueprint for development of our incredible nervous system. We form many memories as we associate sensory experiences with emotions.

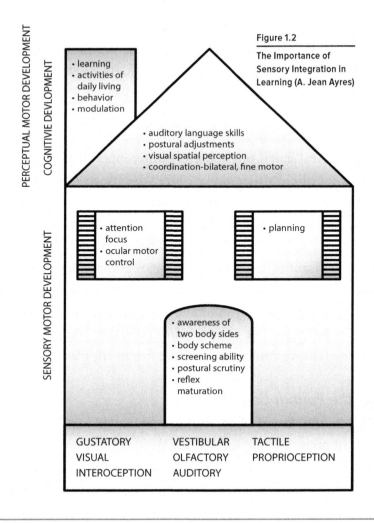

Figure 1.2

The Importance of
Sensory Integration in
Learning (A. Jean Ayres)

The different areas in the nervous system depend on sensation to connect. Once connected, the different areas of the nervous system become more proficient at working together. We use all parts of our nervous system when we learn.

Our relationship with gravity and the early connections among sensory experiences, emotion, and attention contribute to further maturity. We learn that we have two sides to our body and we learn how to coordinate both sides in a task. For example, we can hold our paper with one hand while we write with the other. As we experience success using both sides of our body, we develop our ability to plan our actions and focus our attention. Our movement patterns become more complex; we can play tennis, sew a skirt, draw a tree, and cook brownies. As we experience success, we engage our emotional system. It feels good to succeed at a task; therefore, we are motivated to pay more attention to any task and learn how to maintain our emotions in a calm, alert state so that we can complete our tasks.

Our speech develops as we hear sounds and process the different combinations of sounds. Our vision develops and we build visual perception and visual motor and eye-hand coordination skills. We learn the differences between "cat" and "cap," for example, and we see the difference in the last letter of each word. We then learn how to draw the differences so that we can spell words accurately and write down our ideas!

As we learn to perform tasks and new skills, we develop concentration, organization, self-esteem, self-control, confidence, abstract thought and reasoning, and academic learning.

When sensory processing works efficiently, we can develop many skills, have many successes, and develop the maturity in our regulation skills to continue our learning and our relationships.

Sensory Processing Disorder—SPD

Sensory processing does not always work efficiently. For some people, sensory information can be overwhelming, may not make sense, or may not be interpreted efficiently. Sensory processing depends on the maturation of the nervous system and having lots of wonderful sensory experiences. It also depends on meeting physical needs like getting good sleep and good nutrition. Sensory processing also depends on our emotional state. When we are calm and alert, we can process sensation, and when we succeed in processing sensation, we feel calm and alert. It is a real dynamic where one function depends on the other. Awareness of all the functions and an understanding of the interdependence of the functions enable us to appreciate how complex and wonderful we all are!

Many amazing occupational therapists, psychologists, teachers, parents, doctors, and researchers have contributed to our knowledge of sensory processing.

Dr. Lucy Miller is one of the wonderful occupational therapists who has studied sensory processing for many years. Dr. Lucy has dedicated her career to helping people better understand sensory processing so that children and adults with sensory processing disorder can be identified and supported. Our knowledge of sensory processing and sensory processing disorders is growing. It is a very exciting time!

SPD—A Classification

Dr. Lucy divided sensory processing difficulties into three main areas:

- Sensory modulation disorders
- Sensory discrimination disorders
- Sensory-based postural disorders

Let's learn a little about each type of sensory processing disorder.

Sensory Modulation Disorders

Sensory modulation disorders (SMDs) include sensory over-responders (SOR), sensory under-responders (SUR), and sensory cravers (SS). People who have a sensory modulation disorder can have difficulty regulating their responses to sensation. They may over-respond with a response that is too big, too long, or too quick. A person who under-responds may hardly notice the sensation, may be unaware of the sensation, or may be delayed in responding or respond with less intensity. The sensory craver may constantly seek out the sensation and the need for the sensation never seems to subside. In fact, in sensory cravers, the sensation can create more disorganization.

SOR—Characteristics of the sensory over-responder include:

- Defensive behavior
- Sensory avoider
- Overwhelmed quickly and can become emotional quickly
- Easily goes into fight, flight, or fright mode
- Can have frequent meltdowns
- Tries to control incoming sensation and may appear to be rigid

SUR—Characteristics of the sensory under-responder include:

- Requires intense input just to notice
- Seems to be disinterested and disengaged
- Can be a safety risk due to poor response to pain
- Slow responder

SC—Characteristics of the sensory craver include:

- Constantly seeking sensation
- Bumper and crasher—difficulty controlling body and actions
- Safety concern and can be impulsive

Most children experience both sensory over- and under-responsivity. Their lack of consistency in response can be frustrating for them, their families, their school staff, and their friends.

Sensory Discrimination Disorder—SDD

People with sensory discrimination disorder can have difficulty determining and interpreting differences in the same sensation or even mix up sensations.

SDD—Characteristics of a person with sensory discrimination disorder include:
- Can't differentiate between sensations, even between internal (inside the body) and external (from the environment)
- Can get mixed up between sensations (may hear a colour or taste a number)
- May have difficulty attaching the correct meaning to sensation: where is it coming from, what it means, how to interpret it

Sensory-Based Movement Disorder—SBMD

People with sensory-based movement disorder can have difficulty with planning and sequencing familiar and unfamiliar tasks and with balance and coordination of speech, as well as fine and gross motor skills.

SBMD—Characteristics of a person with sensory-based movement disorder include:

Postural Disorder
- Can have difficulty with core strength, balance, and bilateral co-ordination
- Can have low tone, easy fatigue
- Can have associated responses
- Can be described as a "leaner"

Dyspraxia
- Can be clumsy
- Can have difficulty learning new movements
- Can have difficulty creating new movements (ideational praxis)
- Can have difficulty sequencing movements (ideomotor praxis), even movements that have been practiced before
- May prefer familiar tasks as new ones are difficult to learn
- Can affect motor skills and speech

We can have more than one type of sensory processing disorder and sometimes we may be over-responsive in one sensation and under-responsive in another. We can even be over/under-responsive while processing one sensation! Remember that sensory processing is a function of our nervous system. Our physical state (sleep, nutrition, growth), our emotional state (excitement, fear, support), the demands placed on us, and our amount of stress can have a big impact on our ability to process sensation.

The Stages of Sensory Processing

We can also look at the stages of sensory processing that we all experience:

We *register* the sensation—We become aware of the change in sensation: *I smell a new smell!*

We *orient* to the sensation—We pay attention to the sensation. *That is a delicious smell! I want to know more about it!*

We *integrate* the sensation—We put all the sensory information together to form the whole picture of what we are experiencing: *That delicious smell is also warm and coming from the kitchen.*

We *interpret* the sensation—We attach meaning to the sensation. The meaning is derived from our previous knowledge and experiences, our memories, and we attach a feeling to the meaning: *The delicious smell is bread! Woo hoo; I love fresh, warm bread!*

We *organize* our response to the sensation—We can ignore, avoid, or engage in the sensation: *Mom, can I have some of that delicious bread?*

We cannot prepare a functional response if we have difficulty registering, orienting, integrating, interpreting, or organizing our response. The ability to process sensation is key to knowing that there is a request, orienting to it, putting all the information together (paying attention to what is important and ignoring what is not), attaching meaning, and planning our response.

Anyone can have difficulty processing sensation and may experience the world as a very unpredictable place. It is estimated that 5% to 16% of children show signs of sensory processing disorder. This means that in every 100 children, 5 to 16 will have difficulty processing sensation. At least one child in each classroom will need understanding and support (Ahn, Miller et al., 2004; Ben-Sasoon, Carter et al., 2009).

Chapter Two

Let's Look at the Nervous System

Learning Objectives—
In this chapter, teachers and students will learn:

- Communication in the nervous system
- Insulation of the nervous system
- Three nervous systems that work together—central, peripheral, and autonomic
- Sympathetic overdrive
- The sensory systems—vestibular, tactile, olfactory auditory, gustatory, proprioception, vision, and interoception
- Tracts of the spinal cord
- Lobes and functions

Our nervous system is truly magnificent! Imagine millions of neurons firing together, bringing sensory information into the brain. The sensory information is filtered and sorted and a motor response is chosen to meet the demand of the environment. The work of the nervous system is amazing and most of the time it happens without our awareness!

Sensory Detectives, welcome to the learning journey of the nervous system—a complex and wonderful system that has many parts. Understanding the nervous system helps us appreciate all the work that goes into sensory processing, planning responses, managing emotions, and choosing behaviors. Let's put on our detective hats to figure out how the process of sensory integration actually occurs.

When we learn about sensory processing, it is helpful to learn about the individual sensory inputs first; then we can learn how the individual sensations join and are processed together to give us information about our environment and ourselves. Senses are ALWAYS processed together and they are always processed with attention and emotion. For example, when we hear a robin singing in a tree, our auditory (hearing) sense picks up a different sound, our attention is harnessed around this event, our eyes look up to see if we can find what is making the new sound, and our vestibular system provides input to the muscles to stabilize our head so that we can move our eyes and keep our balance. Our proprioception system gives us information about the position of our body. We are interested in what is making this beautiful sound and our emotional system is engaged. When we are interested and motivated to participate in an action, the neurochemistry in our brain facilitates communication between the brain's neurons and structures. We combine information from all the senses, mix in attention and motivation, and thus we can process the information and attach meaning to the event. The robin is singing … spring has arrived!

Sensory Detectives, let's begin by learning about our marvelous nervous system.

Communication in the Nervous System

We have three main types of systems in our nervous system: central, peripheral, and autonomic. These systems work together to maintain our health and our functioning. These systems communicate via nerves and chemicals. Each nerve has a cell body with many dendrites attached. These dendrites have docking stations that receive chemical messages from other neurons in the chemical soup that surrounds the whole nervous system. This "soup" is called cerebral spinal fluid. When the dendrites pick up a message, the nerve cell depolarizes, or changes

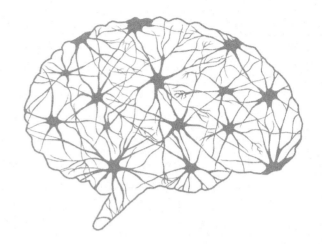

its charge, and an electrical charge is created. This electrical charge travels down the axon—or tail—of the neuron. When the charge reaches the end of the axon, it excites the end plates to release the message chemically. The chemicals enter a gap between the neurons called a synaptic gap and connect to the docking stations of the next neuron to depolarize (change the electrical charge) it and changes the chemical message into an electrical one again.

 Sensory Detectives, that is a lot of work! You do that work without even thinking about it! Isn't that incredible?

Insulation of the Nerves That Work Together

When our neurons practice communicating that we have experienced a sensation or executed a motor response, we can insulate the connections with a substance called myelin. Myelin surrounds all the neurons involved in the sensory processing or motor response and supports the communication of messages because it surrounds the nerves with an insulating layer.

 Sensory Detectives, do you know that insulation protects the messages so that they will not be lost or fizzle out when many messages are coming into the brain at the same time?

We have many millions of myelinated tracts in our nervous system. The more myelination a tract of neurons has, the faster and more efficient the processing and communication between the neurons becomes.

All these tracts, or connections within the nervous system, resemble a car that has many wires. Some wires go from the ignition box to the engine and other wires go from the steering wheel to the steering column. Some wires go to the ignition, others to the windows, the radio, and the windshield wipers. These wires are covered with an *insulating* plastic, like myelin, that helps the wire hold the charge and communicate with other wires and the car's equipment. Although each wire has a different starting point, ending point, and function, they all work together to make the car function and move.

Sensory Detectives, we have learned only a little about the nervous system and how the individual neurons communicate. Put on your seat belts, the ride into the nervous system is full of twists and turns! The nervous system is made up of three different parts that work together so that the body functions. Let's learn about the three systems that make up the nervous system: the central, peripheral, and autonomic nervous systems.

Three Parts of the Nervous System

Central Nervous System

The *central* nervous system is made up of the cortex (brain), the central structures, the limbic system, thalamus, midbrain, brain stem, and spinal cord. It is called the central nervous system because it is in the center of our body. This system is the main control center. It accepts information from the sensory systems, processes that sensation, processes emotion, pays attention, and organizes motor responses. A part of our brain, called the frontal lobe, has many connections to our brain stem and limbic system (home of our emotions). These connections enable what are called executive functions. Executive functions help us regulate our motor responses and our behavior so that we can behave and respond in a way that matches our environment. We'll learn more about these functions in Chapters 5 and 6. The central nervous systems can also store memories of events and movements. Sometimes motor—or movement—memories are so well stored that we can perform a movement without paying attention. For example, you may hang your coat in your cubbie, but you may not remember doing it because the act is such a practiced action that you didn't need to pay attention.

 Sensory Detectives, do you remember getting dressed this morning? Do you remember getting on the school bus? You may not remember these actions because they are so well practiced that you can do them automatically! Are you ready for the journey of sensation? Here we go!

The Journey of Sensation

Let's look at the journey of sensation. It is really marvelous!

Your ears pick up the sound of a person speaking in your environment. This auditory information is combined with other information. Your eyes give you information about who is speaking. You combine the auditory and visual information with your body position (vestibular, proprioceptive, and tactile systems) to determine where the speaker is in relation to you and if the speaker is actually speaking to you.

All this information from the auditory, visual, vestibular, proprioceptive, and tactile systems is carried up to the central nervous system via nerves and gathers together in the brain stem (which sits right at the top of the spinal cord). Our attention helps us determine which information that is brought into our central nervous system is important and which information we can ignore. We like our teacher and enjoy interacting with her so our emotional system is engaged and this supports our attention. We focus on the teacher's voice and can ignore the student who is coughing and the sound of students running in the hall.

Neuroscience research continually provides information about how the brain works and how the systems actually work together. When our emotional system is engaged to support our attention to support the processing of sensory information, a special chemical soup is thought to form. The chemicals in this soup enable nerves to connect and communicate so that the messages continue through the different structures of the brain. If we are not interested in math or not motivated to interact with our teacher, if we cannot make sense of the sensory messages, the chemical soup that is created does not have the necessary ingredients to enable the nerves to communicate messages and the message can be lost.

If we were to pay attention to all the information we receive at any moment, we would be overwhelmed by the tsunami of information. We would feel constantly bombarded with messages and may be unable to respond to any of them. This is what can happen if the nervous system is hyper-responsive to sensation. People who are hyper-responsive to sensation can feel as if they are in a busy, crowded, loud, hot, flashy shopping mall on a busy shopping day all the time. They can feel exhausted and irritated because they cannot screen out sensation; their nervous systems may feel as if they are constantly being bombarded with sensation.

Our emotional system helps our attention focus on what is important to us and enables us to ignore all the rest of the sensation that is not important. Students who are hyper-responsive can use their focus to help them screen out competing sensory information so they are not overwhelmed. When they focus on what they enjoy, for example, they may not hear you calling their name or notice that the class has left to go to the library!

We are always learning about our nervous system, how we work and what strategies can help us work better. Neuroscience research can give us answers to the questions we have about our nervous system. This field of research is exciting! It's fun to learn how we work.

Sensory Detectives, let's find out how sensory information comes into the peripheral nervous system.

Peripheral Nervous System

The *peripheral* nervous system carries information to and from the periphery—or outer edges—of the body. The peripheral nervous system has two parts: sensory nerves that bring information into the central nervous system from the body and motor nerves that carry commands from the central nervous system to the muscles and organs. The peripheral and central nervous system must work together to support functioning.

For example, when Annie does her finger-painting in art, the peripheral sensory system brings her brain information about the texture of the paint, the edges of the paper, her posture, and the position of her body in relation to the paint and paper. The vision, auditory, and olfactory systems bring in information about the color and shine of the paint, the sound of the paint sloshing over the paper, and the wet smell of the paint on the paper. All the sensations combine in the central nervous system to give Annie the information she needs to organize her motor response. Her motor system has many memories of movements that Annie can organize and send to her peripheral motor neurons. The job of the peripheral motor neurons is to carry the message to muscles so that they move to perform a function—finger-paint! When the information is processed well and Annie plans and executes her motor response accurately, she can succeed in finger-painting and enjoy the activity! Her memory of the task can include the motor sequence and the emotional imprint of feelings of success and fun.

 Sensory Detectives, we have learned about the central and peripheral nervous systems. Now, let's explore the third system, the autonomic nervous system.

Autonomic Nervous System

The third part of our nervous system is called the *autonomic* nervous system. This system works automatically, without our even thinking about it. The autonomic system takes care of our body's health. It is in charge of our digestion and elimination (going to the toilet). It also cares for our eyes and makes sure they have lots of water around them so that the lids can close easily and they can be healthy. The change in the size of the pupil in response to light is a function of the autonomic nervous system. The autonomic nervous system kicks into gear when we get a cut. It organizes the body to clean up the area and sends special cells into the area to mend the sides of the cut with a scar to hold the wound closed. Our cycles of sleep/awake, hunger/thirst, and growth are also organized by our autonomic nervous system. This system is extremely important in keeping us healthy and well.

The autonomic nervous system is made up of two parts: the sympathetic and parasympathetic systems. The sympathetic system is the stronger of the two and is quick to engage. This system engages when we are overwhelmed with sensation, when we are stressed, and when we are experiencing strong emotions. We have three options when we are in sympathetic overdrive: fight, flight, or fright. The parasympathetic system is in charge of our resting, health and digesting. The third part of our autonomic nervous system is our enteric system. It is the marvelous network of nerves that innervates the gastrointestinal system (stomach and intestines). It works mostly by itself and communicates with the central nervous system.

It is interesting that the body has an autonomic nervous system. Sensory Detectives, do you know that this system is programmed in our nervous system for our survival? It was developed long ago. There are no longer saber-tooth tigers hunting and hoping to eat us for lunch, but the fight, flight, or fright responses remain programmed in our nervous system today. We use these big responses of fight, flight, or fright when we are overwhelmed by too much sensation, too much emotion, or too much demand. Let's learn how the fight, flight, or fright responses can be expressed in school.

Assume that Andrew often kicks the child in front and behind him in line. He is very sensitive to touch and does not want the child in front of or behind him to touch him. He is so afraid of this that he kicks the children before they can even touch him. Andrew may be overwhelmed by touch, even the thought of unexpected touch, and he may choose a *fight* behavior to cope with the sensation. This *fight* behavior can be his autonomic, overwhelmed sympathetic response.

In another example, Joseph does not like strange smells and often runs out of the cafeteria at school. Joseph may be in the *flight* state of an overwhelmed sympathetic response.

Also, Ben often seems to get "stuck" at the entrance of the gym. He is afraid of the noises. He cannot enter the gym or walk away. Ben may be in the *fright* state of an overwhelmed sympathetic response.

Sensory Detectives, when you see a behavior that looks aggressive, like Andrew's kicks, or is unexpected, like Joseph running out of the cafeteria or Ben standing frozen in the gym entrance; it may be a sympathetic response to being overwhelmed by sensation.

Sensory Detectives know that often more than one reason accounts for the behaviors that are expressed. Sensory Detectives understand that some people's nervous system can react to sensation in a big way!

Sympathetic Overdrive

It is not fun to be in sympathetic overdrive; it is an extremely stressed state. We are designed so that we can avoid the activity or sensation that causes our nervous system to be so uncomfortable. The body can react in many ways. It may react physically. Your tummy can hurt, you may get a headache, or you may feel sweaty or nauseous. It can also react with emotions. You may feel angry or frustrated. In addition, you may feel frightened to meet new people or try new things. You may also react with your behaviors. You may run away, hit someone, or not be able to move or speak.

All three systems (central, peripheral, and autonomic) work together to help us stay healthy and function. If one of these systems is not working well, it can have a negative effect on the other systems. For example, if we are having difficulty screening out sensory information and feel constantly bombarded by information, we can feel very stressed. If we cannot remove ourselves from this overwhelmed state of sensation, the ongoing stress can have a terrible impact on our autonomic nervous system and our immune system. We can have difficulty staying healthy. We can have trouble sleeping, we may not feel hungry, we may have tummy aches and headaches, and we may take longer to get better after we catch a cold or experience another sickness.

Sensory Detectives, now that we have an understanding of the whole nervous system, let's go back and look at the individual sensory systems. Can you determine the differences in sensation? Let's learn how to read the clues!

The Sensory Systems

Some sensory systems carry information to the brain via cranial nerves. This means that the nerves are inside the cranium, or head. The cranial nerves carry information from the head and are connected directly to the brain. Other sensory systems carry information from farther away in the body. These systems connect with the spinal cord and travel up to the brain via spinal tracts. Each tract carries specific sensations and has its own name. It passes through the brain stem and then goes to the brain. It is beautifully complicated! We will begin with the first sensory systems to develop: vestibular, tactile, olfactory, and auditory.

The Vestibular System

Dr. Jean Ayres, the occupational therapist we learned about in Chapter 1, called the vestibular sense the master sense. She was right! The vestibular system has a powerful influence on many functions of our nervous system and other sensations. The vestibular system gives us information so that we know:

- If we are moving or still
- The speed of our movement
- The direction of our movement

 Sensory Detectives, do you know the clues indicating that the vestibular system is working well?

The receptors for the vestibular system are in the inner ear, right inside the outer ear. This system is important and is well protected and contained in a bone called the temporal bone. Inside the inner ear are structures that help us maintain balance and detect movement. The auditory sensory apparatus is also included in the inner ear and enables us to hear.

We have three semi-circular canals, or tubes, in our inner ear and each one has a different position. One is positioned in front, one behind, and one to the side. At the bottom of each of these semi-circular canals is a widened area called an ampula. The canals and ampula are filled with fluid called endolymph fluid. The ampula has tiny hairs inside known as stereocellium; these hairs are thin and flexible and wave in the endolymph fluid like seaweed waves in the water. The brain knows the direction of our movement

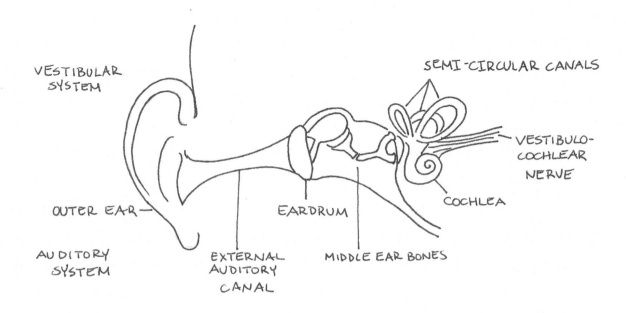

because it can read what the hairs are doing in each inner ear! The brain reads the direction in which the stereocellium are moving and we know the direction of our movement. Other structures are also involved; the utricle tells us about our movement in a horizontal plane (forward and backward, right to left) and the saccule tells us about our movement in a vertical plane (up and down). The information that is transmitted through the vestibular apparatus makes its way to the brain via a cranial nerve called the vestibulo-cochlear nerve. The information is interpreted in many areas of the brain.

Information from the vestibular system has connections with our posture so that we can stay upright against gravity and move our head so that our eyes can follow moving objects. The vestibular system is also connected to our vision, our hearing, and our attention, arousal, and focus. It is a busy system that is turned on all the time!

Parents know the value of the vestibular system and they use rocking to calm their babies and young children and to put their babies to bed.

Teachers, do you know that exercise and movement breaks can help students study and stay alert?

 Who knew the vestibular system was so complex? Amazing! Sensory Detectives, can you find the clues that show the work of the tactile system?

Tactile System

The tactile system is the system of touch. This system helps us determine that something is touching us and the details of what is touching us. For example, we can feel the difference between a scratchy wool sweater and the cool smooth feeling of silk. We use our tactile system to put our hands in our desk and feel the difference between our pencil case and our ruler. Our touch system also tells us about food in our mouth. We can tell the crunchy feeling of popcorn from the smooth feeling of pudding. We use our tactile system to feel the ground under our feet when we walk or run. We can tell the difference between the edge of the stairs when we are walking downstairs and the flat tile of the floor when we reach the bottom of the stairs.

There are many different types of touch receptors. We can determine different textures, pressures, pains, and temperatures. The tactile system is the largest sensory system. It is contained in all of our surfaces, especially the skin. Some parts of our body are very important to our survival and have more tactile receptors per square centimeter than others. For example, the fingertips have more tactile receptors than the back of the hand. We are designed this way so that we can feel items in our hand in great detail, like the pencil you may be holding right now! The tactile receptors send information to the spinal cord, which carries this information via specific tracts to the brain stem and brain so that we can figure out what we are touching or what is touching us.

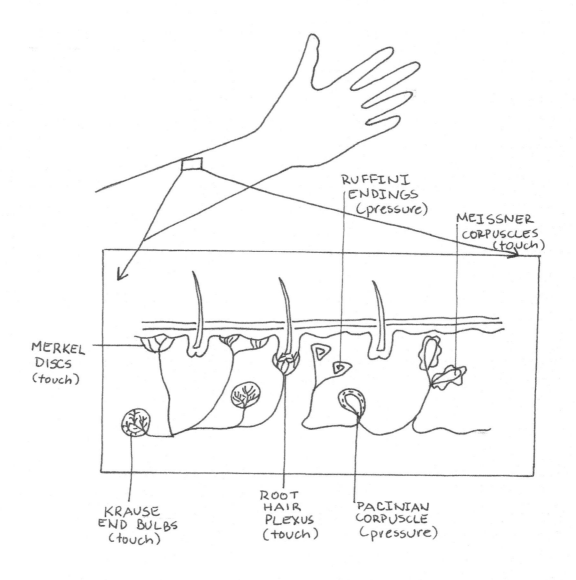

RUFFINI ENDINGS (pressure)

MEISSNER CORPUSCLES (touch)

MERKEL DISCS (touch)

KRAUSE END BULBS (touch)

ROOT HAIR PLEXUS (touch)

PACINIAN CORPUSCLE (pressure)

 Sensory Detectives, we have learned about the vestibular and tactile systems. What do you think are the clues indicating a good smelling system?

Olfactory System

Smell is carried through our olfactory receptors. These receptors are located in the olfactory bulb inside the nose. These bulbs sit on top of the ethmoid bone, which sits behind the nose. The ethmoid bone is filled with holes. It actually looks like coral. The air we breathe contains the chemicals of different smells. These chemicals enter the nose and come in contact with the olfactory receptors. We can smell many hundreds of different smells. Some are pleasant, like the smell of fresh bread, and some are nasty, like the smell of a sewer. Information about smell is carried to the brain by a cranial nerve called the olfactory nerve.

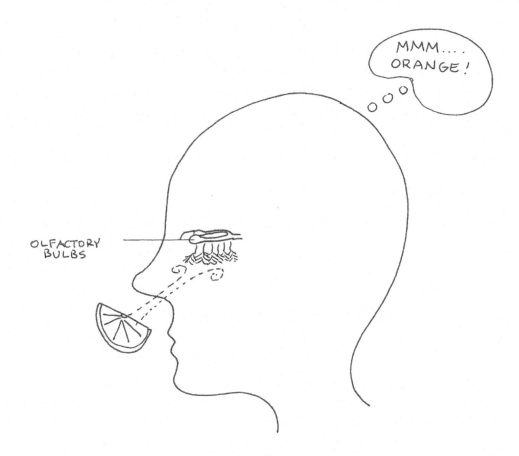

Auditory System

The auditory system can interpret different sounds. We begin to hear before we are even born. We hear our mother's heart beat and digestion sounds before birth and can even respond to familiar voices and music. Babies can recognize sounds that they heard before they were born after they are born, like the voices of their mom and dad.

This system is an engineering masterpiece! A sound travels through the air and when it connects with the eardrum, inside the ear, it vibrates the eardrum. The vibrating eardrum, in turn, vibrates three small bones. They are individually known as the hammer, the anvil, and the stirrup. These bones look like the objects they are named after. These bones vibrate the endolymph in a structure called the cochlea. The cochlea is connected to hair cells, which are connected to a cranial nerve called the vestibulo-cochlear nerve, which carries the auditory information to the temporal lobe of the brain. Remember that this nerve also carries information from the vestibular sense, our master sense.

For an illustration of the auditory system, please see "The Vestibular System" on page 24.

Sensory Detectives, we have learned about the sensory systems that are working before and at birth to help us identify important people who care for us and help us eat so that we can survive. Let's learn clues about the sensory systems that develop after birth, where there is a significant pull of gravity that we need to push against and light that enables us to see.

The vestibular, auditory, tactile, and olfactory sensory systems are ready to deliver information to the brain when we are born. We are designed this way so that we can recognize our parents through smell, sound, and touch. We are also able to know when we are close to our food through smell and touch, and we can orient our head to our food source because the vestibular system gives us the information to position our head.

Other senses develop as we gain experience in the world outside our mom. We develop our ability to taste things, see, know our body's position, and feel our internal state. Let's learn more.

Gustatory System

The gustatory receptors carry information about what we taste. We can taste many combinations of sweet, sour, salty, and bitter. These receptors are located on the tongue, the roof of the mouth, and the insides of the cheeks. Gustatory information is carried to the brain by the gustatory nerve.

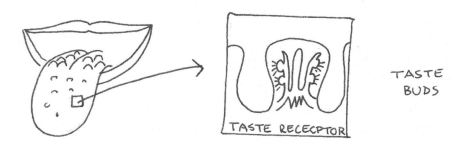

Proprioception System

The proprioception receptors give us information that helps us know the position of our body and the amount of pressure we are using in our movement. Proprioception uses many sensory systems. We have an unconscious awareness of our body's position in space that we use when we are assuming different postures like sitting and standing and when we are performing automatic movement patterns like walking. We can maintain our posture and walking without even thinking. We can even change our position while we focus on the task we are performing. For example, we can move over when our friend wants to sit beside us on the bus. We also have a conscious awareness of our body position. We use this awareness when we

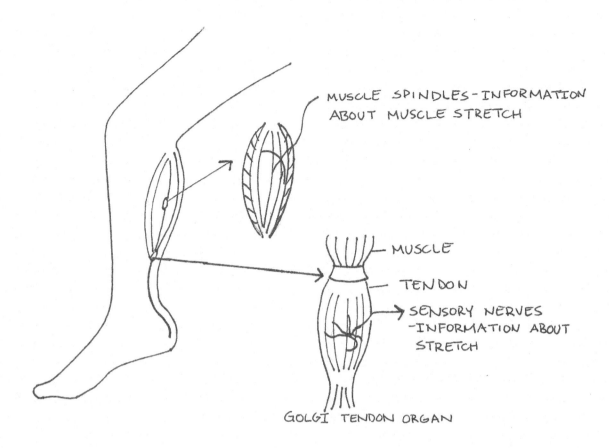

MUSCLE SPINDLES – INFORMATION ABOUT MUSCLE STRETCH

MUSCLE

TENDON

SENSORY NERVES – INFORMATION ABOUT STRETCH

GOLGI TENDON ORGAN

learn a new movement, like how to fold a kootie catcher, or learn to do a lay-up shot in basketball. As movements become better learned, they become more automatic and require less thinking, or conscious control.

Proprioception receptors are located in our joints, skin, and muscles. They are located in all the structures that enable us to move: muscle fibers, ligaments, and joint capsules. These receptors fire when we begin and end movement and can become quiet if we don't change position for a while. Proprioception receptors get better at carrying information about our body position when we understand the pull of gravity. Information from the proprioception receptors travels up the spinal cord, in specific tracts, to reach the brain.

Vision System

The vision system is the sensory system that uses the most energy. The receptor for the vision system is the eye. It takes in light through the pupil and this light shines on the back of the eye on a sensitive band of light receptors in the retina. We have two types of specialized light cells: rods and cones. Rods carry information about the edges of objects and movement and cones carry information about color and detail. Information from the rods and cones is carried to the brain by a cranial nerve called the optic nerve. This amazing nerve divides behind the nose in a place called the optic chiasm and half of the right optic nerve goes to the left side of the brain and half of the left optic nerve goes to the right side of the brain. Wow! What a design!

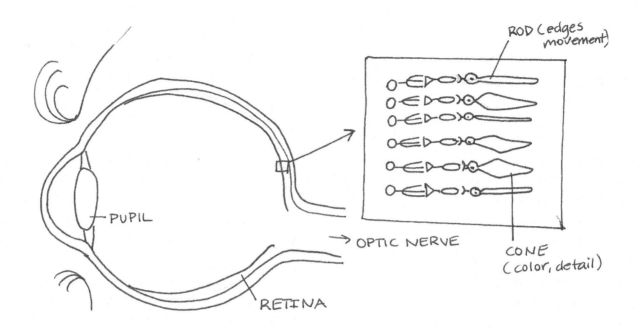

 Sensory Detectives, you have learned lots of information about many of the sensory systems. There is one more … interoception. This is the most studied sensory system right now. Information from within our body gives us clues about what our body needs and what we are feeling. When we know how to interpret interoception information, Sensory Detectives, we can choose what we need to do to stay calm and alert.

Interoception System

The interoception receptors provide information about the world inside you. The interoception system is made up of many different types of receptors. Some are under unconscious control, such as the chemical receptors in our circulation system, which read the levels of salt in our blood and signal us to feel thirsty to balance the salt levels. The pressure-sensitive receptors in our bladder signal that it is time to use the toilet. The stretch receptors in our stomach signal that we are hungry. Our breathing rate and heart rate are in response to the demand for oxygen signaled by chemoreceptors.

We can also feel the effect of emotions in our body, thanks to interoreceptors. Emotions influence the way we feel and how our body is working. For example, when we feel afraid, our sympathetic system can go into sympathetic overdrive and the body doesn't work on digestion, or thinking. All the energy and blood supply are directed to the eyes to see, the legs to run away, and the arms to defend. When we feel afraid, our hands may become sweaty, we may breathe more heavily, and our legs may feel jittery. The tactile, proprioception, and interoception sensations may occur secondary to the effect of the emotion of fear.

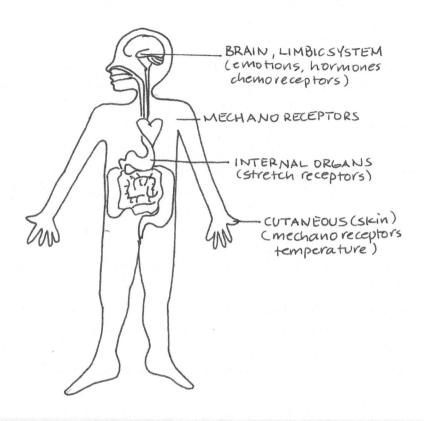

 Sensory Detectives, do you remember the clues to reading the fight, flight, and fright response of an overwhelmed sympathetic response?

The interoception receptors relay information through different tracts to reach the brain. The parts of the brain involved in the interoception system are the limbic system, autonomic nervous system (especially the vagus nerve), the temporal region, and the frontal region. The interoception system links the body's internal state, emotions, cognitive functions, and sense of self. Research is continually discovering new receptors and new facts about the interoception system.

 Sensory Detectives, in Chapters 5 and 6 we will learn sensory and cognitive strategies to support our nervous system to combat the overdrive response to too much sensation, too much emotion, and/or too much demand so that we can maintain a calm state in our nervous system. How does the sensory information make its way from the sensory receptor to the brain? Sensory Detectives, read on!

Spinal Cord Tracts

The spinal cord has sensory tracts that carry information up to the brain. If the name of the tract begins with the word spino, it is a sensory tract because it begins in the spinal cord and carries information up to the brain.

There are three main sensory tracts:

- Posterior columns carry discriminative touch (detail touch), pressure, and vibration.
- Anterior and lateral spinothalamic tracts carry basic touch, temperature, and pain.
- Anterior, lateral, and posterior spinocerebellar tracts carry subconscious proprioception, which is processed without us even thinking about it.

The motor tracts carry instructions for movements from the brain to the muscles or organs. Motor tracts end in the word spinal because they end in the spinal cord.

There are two main groups of motor tracts:

- Anterior and lateral corticospinal tracts carry voluntary motor messages.
- Rubrospinal, anterior and lateral reticulospinal, olivespinal, vestibulospinal, and tectospinal tracts carry motor messages for balance and muscle tone.

Neuroplasticity

The cortex puts all the sensory information together and attaches meaning to it. We learn that different parts of the brain are in charge of different functions. This is mostly true, but it is not a rule. Some functions can be represented in more than one place. If we have an injury to one part of the brain, the brain can be plastic, which means it can change to accommodate a new function. For example, if a person becomes blind, the part of the brain that usually processes visual information can change jobs and learn how to process touch information or auditory information.

 Sensory Detectives, did you know that different areas of the brain are responsible for different functions? Although this is mostly true, it is not always true. Many functions can be stored in more than one place.

Lobes and Functions

In general, the frontal lobe is our lobe of thinking and planning. This lobe contains our executive functions and our motor planning abilities and memories.

The temporal lobes are the lobes of language and speech.

The parietal lobes house the association cortex and this is where the sensory clues and the meaning associated with these sensory clues come together.

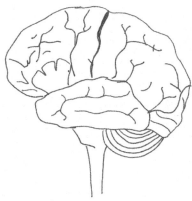

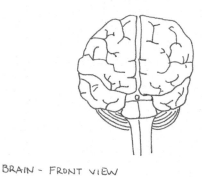

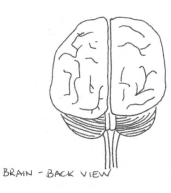

BRAIN - FRONT VIEW

BRAIN - BACK VIEW

BRAIN - SIDE VIEW

The occipital lobe processes vision.

We also have a limbic system, which is where we process emotion. The limbic system is important for learning as we attach meaning to the facts we learn.

The cerebellum helps us balance and maintain our posture. The brain stem and thalamus coordinate incoming and outgoing messages. The brain is a very busy organ, especially in school!

It is also important to understand that all the parts of the brain work together. The sensory information we process can affect our emotions, our cognition, our executive functions, and our behavior. Our emotions can affect our sensory processing, our cognition, our executive functions, and our behavior. Everything can affect everything else. It is important to be aware of our sensory processing as it can have a big effect on our other functions. We will learn about our own sensory processing in Chapter 4.

Putting It All Together

We have learned that:
- We always process many sensations at the same time.
- The central, peripheral, and autonomic nervous systems are in constant contact with each other.
- The sensory systems bring information up to the brain, where it is interpreted.
- Sensory processing, emotions, and cognition are all connected and affect each other.
- The interoception system has many connections among different receptors in the body, body functions, emotions, and cognition.

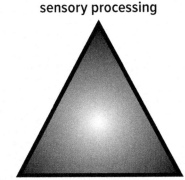

sensory processing

emotion

behavior

Well done, Sensory Detectives! That was a lot of information that you are going to need to perform the detective work in Chapter 3. You will discover:

- How to assess sensory processing in the environment, in interactions with others, and in activities
- How difficulty with sensory processing can be expressed in our physical body, our behavior, and our physiology
- How sensory processing ability can change in response to our environment, our health, the demands that are placed on us, and our emotions

Let's learn!

Chapter Three

Assessment

What Happens When It Is Difficult to Process Sensation?

Learning Objectives—
In this chapter, teachers and students will learn:

- The definition of sensory processing disorder
- The definition of function and occupation
- Classification of SPD by Dr. Winnie Dunn
- Classification of SPD by Dr. Lucy Miller
- Signs of a disregulated nervous system
- How to observe behaviors using a sensory lens
- Assessing SPD
- A sensory approach and activities
- Professionals who can help

Hello again, Sensory Detectives! Congratulations on all your learning in Chapter 2. Chapter 3 is about sensory processing disorder (SPD). We will look at what happens when sensation is not processed efficiently or effectively. You will learn the clues to watch for to identify SPD in yourself and your classmates.

Sensory Processing Disorder—SPD

How do we know when we have difficulty processing sensation? Research suggests that 5% to 16% (Ahn, Miller et al., 2004; Ben-Sasoon, Carter et al., 2009) of students experiences sensory processing difficulties. Sensory processing disorder refers to the inability of the nervous system to process sensation effectively.

We all occasionally have difficulty processing sensation. For example, if we are tired, we may not be able to effectively feel the buttons of our shirt as we dress in the morning. If we are frustrated about losing in a board game, we may not be able to effectively control the pressure we exert through our game piece and the whole game may go flying! People who have SPD can have difficulty processing sensation most of the time, not just when they are tired or frustrated. The difficulties they experience can look different in different environments or on different days.

Assume that Shayna has difficulty keeping her body still when she sits in a reading circle except for the days she has gym. On gym days, her body is able to get all the movement (proprioceptive and vestibular sensation) it needs to feel organized and calm and she is able to sit still.

It is challenging to have difficulties in processing sensation. It takes a lot of energy to manage and cope with all the sensations and regulate our responses, emotions, and behavior. The challenges may not be consistent. However, one day or one environment may offer the sensation to help the nervous system stay calm and organized, like gym days for Shayna. The difficulties are real and when we understand how to recognize the challenges, we can support the nervous system with sensation. Let's learn about the clues students may show when sensation is difficult to process.

 Sensory Detectives, when is difficulty processing a sensation a sensory processing disorder?

When difficulty with sensory processing constantly interferes with function, it can be considered sensory processing disorder. If it doesn't interfere with function, it can be considered a dysregulated nervous system that has trouble processing sensation in that moment.

Function—It's What We Do!

Function is the ability to plan and respond to a request from the environment or a task demand in a successful way. The role and occupation of a student is to learn. Our occupation is our role, our profession, our job. Supporting sensory

processing can support the function of the student—learning (www.thefreedictionary.com/function)!

Many students can have mild sensory processing difficulties and still adapt to maintain success in their function. For example, the student who needs the vestibular and proprioception sensation of movement can ask to go get a drink many times a day. This behavior is functional and the students can maintain their occupation as a student.

When sensory processing difficulties are too severe and students cannot get their sensory needs met in the classroom environment, their behavior may inhibit their ability to function and they may not succeed in their occupation as a student.

 Onward, Sensory Detectives! Let's learn about the types of SPD and the clues that we can see.

Classification of Dr. Winnie Dunn

Different classification systems have been created by knowledgeable occupational therapists. Dr. Winnie Dunn created a system that divides nervous systems into those that are hyper-responsive to sensation and reach the overload point very quickly. These nervous systems have a low threshold. A low threshold means that it doesn't take much sensation to overwhelm the person's nervous system. The word threshold means the entrance to a room. A low threshold is flat, which makes it easy to enter a room. From a sensory processing perspective, a low threshold means that sensation can easily enter and overwhelm the nervous system. Let's look at some examples:

Joanne hates the playground equipment and will not participate in climbing or any activity where her feet are off the ground. She can be described as hyper-responsive to vestibular sensation.

Taniqua always rubs the place on her arm where her friends bump into her in line. She hates arts and crafts and anything that feels wet and sticky. Taniqua can be described as hyper-responsive to tactile sensation.

Cassy covers her ears in the gym. She cannot catch a ball because her hands are always covering her ears. Cassy can be described as hyper-responsive to auditory sensation.

Arvinder squeezes her nose and tries to smell her pencils during class. She smells her pencils more often during lunch when the smells of her classmates' lunches fill the air. She can be described as hyper-responsive to olfactory sensation.

Ramesh often squeezes his eyes shut and squints when he is in the hall, the library, or the art room. He prefers to read from his reader under the desk where it is darker. He can be described as hyper-responsive to visual sensation.

Fred rarely tries new foods. He agrees to taste one of the samosas that his friend Dupti brings in to celebrate her birthday. The samosa has an unfamiliar spice in it. Fred runs for water even though the spice is not hot and wipes his tongue with a paper towel. He can be described to be hypersensitive to gustatory sensation.

It is rare for people to be hyper-responsive to proprioceptive information. Proprioception is often used to help calm the nervous system. If a person is sensitive to proprioceptive input, they will avoid activities where they feel deep touch or pressure and may even avoid changing the position of their body.

Paula constantly needs to use the toilet. The stretching sensation of her bowel and bladder is painful to her. Paula can be described as hypersensitive to interoception sensation.

Sensory Detectives, did you notice that hyper-responsiveness is easy to spot? The behavior has a definite goal of ending the activity. It is often accompanied by an emotional response, which is usually fear. Let's look at the other extreme—hypo-responsiveness.

When people are hypo-responsive to sensation, they don't seem to notice the sensation and seem to require a lot of the sensation to notice it. Such a person can be described as having a high threshold. A high threshold means that it takes a lot of sensation for the person's nervous system to notice that a sensory event has occurred. Remember that the word threshold means the entrance to a room. A high threshold is like a wall that a person has to climb over to enter the room. From a sensory processing perspective, a high threshold means that it takes a lot of sensation to capture the person's attention! Let's look at some examples:

Levy is always on the go! He loves movement and always plays on swings, hoops, and ropes in the playground. He can be described as hypo-responsive to vestibular sensation.

Brian is constantly dropping his pencil. He doesn't seem to feel it in his hand. After lunch, he often wears some of his sandwich on his cheeks because he just doesn't notice it. Brian can be described as hypo-responsive to tactile sensation.

The teacher can call Jaden's name many times in a busy classroom and Jaden does not seem to notice. Jaden can be described as hypo-responsive to auditory sensation.

Giacomo likes to throw paper in the air and watch it fall. He also enjoys spilling water and looking at the reflections in the water's surface. He can be described as hypo-responsive to visual sensation.

Gina often puts her nose in to smell the garbage, the lunch bags, the markers, and anything else that has a strong smell. She can be described as hypo-responsive to olfactory sensation.

Frieda puts everything in her mouth! She puts stones, sand, and glue in her mouth and she loves spicy food. Frieda can be described as hypo-responsive to gustatory sensation.

Omar loves to lean on his friends during reading circle. When he walks down the hall he likes to roll his body along the wall. Omar loves to carry heavy things like books and he loves pushing open the door for his friends. Heavy work offers a lot of proprioception sensation and Omar can be described as hypo-responsive to proprioception sensation.

Polly often becomes irritable close to lunchtime. When she is hungry, she can be grumpy. Polly cannot feel her empty tummy and responds to the interoception sensation with her emotion and behavior. She can be described as being hypo-responsive to interoception sensation.

 Sensory Detectives, did you notice that people with a hypo-responsive reaction to sensation often seek out the sensation? Their nervous system seems to need the sensation. They can use their behavior to seek it out. Sometimes other sensations don't make sense so people can seek out a sensation they can process. Sometimes people are so sensitive to sensation that they shut down (remember the fright state of sympathetic overdrive?). These people seem to be hypo-responsive, but they may actually be hyper-responsive and in shut-down. It can be complicated!

Classification by Dr. Lucy Miller

Dr. Lucy Miller has dedicated her life to helping people recognize and treat SPD. She developed a classification system that considers the hyper and hypo response to sensation under a heading called sensory modulation disorder (SMD). Dr. Miller reminds us that some people's nervous system can move between hyper- and hypo-responsiveness. This can make sensory experiences unpredictable. A third subtype of SMD is called the sensory seeker. This person has a nervous system that craves sensation but never seems to be satisfied.

The second main subtype of Dr. Miller's classification is sensory discrimination disorder. In this subtype, the nervous system has difficulty attaching the correct meaning to the sensation and cannot discriminate subtle differences between sensations. This subtype of SPD can be confusing!

The third subtype of SPD, sensory-based movement disorder (SBMD), has two categories. One relates to posture, balance, and the ability to move accurately. The other subtype of SBMD is dyspraxia. Praxis is the ability to come up with an idea for a response and put the steps of the response in the correct order. Dyspraxia is a dys-order of praxis. In dyspraxia, the nervous system cannot come up with an accurate response or cannot put all the small steps in the right order, even though the person knows what he or she wants to do. Dyspraxia is one of the most frustrating disorders! You know what you want to do, you remember that you may have done it before, but you can't organize a response. This can happen in movement or in speech and language.

Sensory Detectives, you may find the classification systems complicated. Occupational therapists study SPD for many years to understand the disorder and still have lots of questions! Many research studies are currently looking at SPD, assessments, and treatments. Research will influence and guide changes to the classification systems of SPD. While we are waiting for this, we can look for clues that may suggest that someone is having difficulty interpreting sensation. What are the body's clues that a student may have difficulty processing sensation and may have difficulty with regulation?

Signs of a Disregulated Nervous System

The body is very smart and will express when it is not comfortable. The physical body can express stress in many ways. The autonomic nervous system, which we learned about in Chapter 2, can go into overload due to stress. Stress can be from difficulty processing sensation, task demands, social difficulties, or physical challenges. Below are clues to watch for.

Signs of overload in the autonomic nervous system include:

- Yawning
- Sneezing/hiccoughing
- Sweating
- Gagging/spitting up
- Breathing irregularly
- Changing skin color/tone
- Changing state or mood
- Elimination of bowel or bladder (in extreme situations)

Behavioral signs of overload include:

- Fussing/crying
- Grimacing (strained facial expressions)
- Sighing/startling (the "jump" when you are suddenly frightened)
- Stiffening of the muscles
- Averting the gaze (looking away)
- Pushing away
- Arching back
- Zoning out

Sensory Detectives, look at the following case. There are very different responses to the same event. Can you see the clues? Can you see how the responses to the sensation of pizza interfered with the functional response of Claire and Brad?

It's pizza day at school and everyone is excited. When the pizza arrives in the classroom, Claire asks the teacher if she can go to the washroom. "Claire, the pizza is here, don't you want to stay for a piece?" the teacher asks. Claire shakes her head; she is holding her breath and then runs from the room. The teacher remembers that Claire has an extremely sensitive sense of smell and the smell of the pizza overwhelmed her nervous system and she had to leave the room.

Brad almost throws himself into the pizza, even as the words "be careful, it's hot" hang in the air. After chewing for a few seconds, Brad spits the pizza out and grabs for his water to relieve the heat in his mouth. Brad's nervous system is hypo-responsive to the temperature of the pizza and needs a few seconds to process that the temperature was too high.

Both examples of sensory processing disorder highlight a problem with the function of eating pizza. When the nervous system has difficulty processing sensation, there can be a problem in making sense of the sensation and choosing an appropriate response to the sensation. When an incorrect meaning is given to the sensation, the motor response cannot be accurate and function can be impaired. Remember the cake analogy in Chapter 1? The cake will not turn out well if the type and amount of ingredients are incorrect.

Some students in the classroom have been assessed by occupational therapists, doctors, and psychologists and identified as having sensory processing challenges. They will have reports to explain their challenges and strategies to support their function in the classroom. Other students who have sensory processing disorders will not yet have been identified. The key to discovering and supporting these students is observation. When a student is not successful in their function in the classroom, our first response may be that they are "behaving badly." However, very few students choose to behave badly; they are often unable to organize and modulate their responses to sensation or emotion and their function in the classroom suffers.

Sensory Detectives, here is where you get to be a detective! When you see a student who is having difficulty with function, try to figure out why the difficulty is happening.

Observing Behaviors

1. Make the assumption that the child would perform the request if he or she could, but the child can't. Behavior is often a coping strategy or an expression of children's frustration at their lack of success.
2. Use your sensory lens to investigate the behavior:
   - Label the behavior.
   - When does it happen?
   - What prompts it to happen?
   - Who does it happen with?
   - Where does it happen?
   - Why do you think it happens?
   - What strategy do you want to try to see if it decreases the behavior?
   - Did the strategy work?
3. Do you see any clues that the body is stressed?

Let's consider this example: Michelle constantly touches the belongings of the other students. The teacher and students have asked her many times to keep her hands to herself. Michelle has trouble keeping her hands to herself. The attraction to touch new items is so strong and so motivating that she cannot follow the teacher's request. Michelle cannot look at the teacher and she starts to jump up and down.

Sensory Detectives, even though it seems that Michelle isn't listening and obeying the request to keep her hands to herself, we know that there may be another reason why Michelle has to touch everything. We can crack the case! Let's go through the steps:

Label the behavior: Michelle is touching items that don't belong to her.

When does it happen? It seems to happen during classroom transition times, like going from the desk to the circle on the floor, and during times of prolonged sitting.

What prompts it to happen? It seems to be in response to change, which can be stressful, and loss of focus, which can happen when the body is still for a while.

Who does it happen with? Everyone!

Where does it happen? It happens at circle time on the floor, in line, and during waiting and during transitions.

Why do you think it happens? It seems to be a way to maintain attention and body posture/position and a way to cope with change. Michelle seems to seek tactile input to help her nervous system stay calm and alert.

Strategies to try: Make Michelle a sensory pouch with some tactile items and change the items every day so that they stay interesting. Michelle can touch her own objects when she is making a transition or needs to increase her attention.

Did the strategy work? Michelle is distracted by the sensory pouch initially, but within a day she is able to use it effectively. She still touches her friends' objects but much less frequently. It turns out that Michelle can listen better when she is touching something!

Clues of a stressed body: Difficulty with eye contact (decreased visual sensation and minimized perception of the teacher's displeasure) and the need to jump (increased proprioception sensation) may have been ways for Michelle to calm her nervous system

Sensory Detectives, no one discipline has all the answers. Bring in all the great minds in your team—your teacher, fellow students, parents, and school professionals. Students who are having difficulty can also be on the team if they are able. You can approach the case as if you are solving a mystery. Gathering information is the first step. It is important to let the team players know that you are gathering information to discover WHY the child is having difficulty with function. Make it clear that you are not judging the

function as good or bad; it just doesn't match with the classroom environment or the learning success of the student.

Parents are important members of the team. They are experts on their child. Involve the parents in the detective work.

- Does this behavior happen at home?
- When, where, with whom, and why do the parents think the behavior is happening?
- Does the behavior look the same or different at home and at school?

Environments and demands differ between home and school and, therefore, parents and teachers often report different behaviors. This can contribute to a feeling that parents are defending their child or making excuses for their child. It can also contribute to a feeling that teachers cannot manage or motivate the child. We need a common ground from which to work. We need to understand that the nervous system can respond differently to different sensory environments, which can contribute to the differences in function.

Assessing SPD

How do you find a common ground? Working from a similar document or assessment is a good place to begin. Some formal assessments are standardized. This means that they have been used on many students to determine the expected range of performance for each age. These assessments can be graded by an occupational therapist who can also interpret and share the results:

- Sensory Profile
- Sensory Performance Measure (has a school and a home questionnaire so that environments can be compared)
- Sensory Inventory

Informal checklists can be found in books or online. These checklists are not standardized, which means that the scores cannot be compared to other children of the same age. The informal sensory checklists are not graded but can still be helpful in guiding you to look at specific sensory processing challenges. The best assessment involves taking the findings of these informal checklists and/or formal assessments and comparing them to observations of the student's function in different environments, with different people, and with different activities. You will begin to see patterns that can lead you to try strategies to improve

function. Monitor the success of the strategies you try. Are they working? Amazing! Keep it up! Are they not working? No problem; let's come up with new ideas.

It is a process and sometimes it takes a little time to get it right. The student you are supporting will appreciate your efforts.

Many worksheets to encourage collaboration between home and school have been written by other professionals and may support what you find in your sensory checklists. One example of these worksheets is the *Collaborative Problem Solving Worksheet*, written by Dr. Ross Greene. This is a great resource to problem solve around problem behaviors to determine the potential underlying cause(s).

 Sensory Detectives, let's look at some sensory processing challenges and how strategies can be used throughout the day, in different environments, with different teachers and in different subjects.

In the example of Michelle and her need to touch items, we learned that if Michelle has access to items that she can touch, it can decrease her touching of items that belong to her friends. This strategy can be used at circle time in the classroom or at any time she is in one position for an extended period of time. We learned that Michelle is able to listen better when she is touching an item. This strategy can also work during transitions in/out of school and to/from recess, the library, and the gym. Being able to touch items may, for example, help Michelle deal with the change of having a substitute teacher or a new student in her class. Giving Michelle the sensation she is seeking helps her feel calm and regulates her behavior.

Ashley is often overwhelmed by sound. She dislikes the gym even though she loves sports and avoids noisy recess games. Providing Ashley with headphones that block out the extra sound that she can wear in noisy environments can help increase her tolerance for sound. She can wear them during gym, recess, and transitions in the noisy hallways. Another effective strategy for Ashley may be to take away sensation. Giving her the opportunity to calm down and relax in a quiet room/classroom tent with quiet activities a few times during the day may give her the chance to reset her nervous system and be better able to deal with noise. Having quiet time at home before dinner may help Ashley calm down from the demands of her day and muster the energy to deal with the noise during dinner with her family and two noisy little brothers! We don't always have to add sensation opportunities. Sometimes we need to remove sensation and demand for the nervous system to feel calm and regulated. We will learn many strategies to do this in Chapters 5 and 6.

 Sensory Detectives, which teachers and friends make this student feel most comfortable? What are the sensory qualities of the teacher or friend that match the student? Answers to these questions give us more clues about sensory processing strengths and challenges.

A Sensory Approach

We are all walking sensory generators. Some of us speak in loud voices and some are quiet. Some wear clothing with bright colors and patterns and others wear plain clothing. Some smell like a perfume factory and some don't smell at all. We are all different, that is what makes the world so interesting. When a student with sensory processing challenges has a teacher who matches his or her sensory needs, the student is able to feel comfortable, regulate behavior, and function well.

Gloria is very sensitive to loud sounds. She often jumps out of her seat when the bell goes off for recess. She is also very sensitive to visual sensation and often looks out the window at the trees blowing in the breeze because she can find the blackboard and all the art and papers hung up around the blackboard confusing and overwhelming. In second grade, Gloria is placed in Mr. Gregoris' classroom. Mr. Gregoris has a calm and gentle voice. He encourages a quiet classroom and warns students when the bell will ring. He also has a very organized classroom and keeps the walls around the blackboard bare so that there is no competition for visual attention. Gloria's sensitive nervous system feels very comfortable in this classroom. She matches the style of Mr. Gregoris. She is able to feel calm and regulated in his classroom and is able to function well.

Sensory Detectives, you have learned about the importance of observing the sensory environments and the people in those environments. Let's learn about activities. Activities can also give us clues about the ability to process sensation.

Sensory Activities

Observing the activities or subjects that a student does best in can be helpful in determining sensory processing strengths and challenges. When the nervous system feels calm and regulated with movement, students may do best in activities and subjects that incorporate movement, like gym and recess. The movement can be incorporated into stationary activities by offering movable seating like a mambo seat. A mambo seat looks like a mushroom and has a rounded bottom, which enables movement. Shayna, whom we met earlier in this chapter, is most regulated on days when she has gym. Perhaps having gym breaks two or three times during each school day would help Shayna's nervous system feel regulated.

When the nervous system feels calm and regulated with a quiet environment, the student may do best in the library, the chapel, or during tests. Offering headphones that block out noise can enable the student to function in activities that are noisy, like music or gym. Gloria may find headphones helpful when she leaves the classroom to participate in gym or recess.

Michelle loves touching tactile items and feels regulated when she has access to this sensation. Giving her tactile items to touch decreases the behavior of reaching out to touch items that are not hers. Some students avoid touch. They do well with activities like reading and writing and dislike messy wet activities like finger-painting in art. Changing the art activity by putting the finger-paint in a plastic bag or wearing rubber gloves when finger-painting can help the student who has difficulty processing touch succeed in the activity.

We need to see the student underneath the behaviors! It can be extremely discouraging to children to be reprimanded for behaviors that are not under their control. Behaviors that are used to avoid, seek, or help sensation make sense can be misinterpreted as controlling or willful behavior. Empowered with knowledge about sensory processing, we can see the behaviors for what they are and support the nervous system of the child so that he or she can get on with the job of learning.

 Sensory Detectives know that clues can be found in the assessments of other disciplines. We can't stop hunting for clues until we crack the case!

Professionals Who Can Help

Sensory processing is one lens we can use to interpret behavior. There are many reasons for difficulty regulating behavior, emotion, and movement. Don't forget to consider that the person may have difficulty in another area of development. The following chart lists other areas to assess and who can perform the assessment.

Difficulty with	Could be helped by
Speech and language	Speech-language pathologist
Hearing	Audiologist
Vision	Behavioral optometrist, optometrist
Executive functions	Psychologist, occupational therapist
Physical difficulties (sleep, eating, sickness)	Doctor in coordination with alternative medical practitioners, massage therapist
Learning challenges	Special education teacher, tutor
Coordination challenges	Occupational, physical therapist, gym teacher, kinesiologist, personal trainer, adapted physical educator, dance teacher
Social skills	Social worker, occupational therapist, behavior therapist
Behavior regulation	Behavior therapist, occupational therapist

It may seem daunting to perform all the assessments required to determine the underlying reasons for the difficulties students may experience in the classroom. Sometimes assessments are not performed because it seems daunting to add more strategies into an already busy classroom. We have learned over the years that although assessments may be stressful, they help us better understand the underlying reasons for behaviors. Only then can we learn how to support students so that their nervous system can be able to learn more functional behaviors. This is what makes assessments worthwhile.

 Well done, Sensory Detectives! You have learned so much in this chapter about how to identify the clues to detect sensory processing difficulties. You learned that clues can be found by completing sensory checklists and collaborating with parents and professionals. You also discovered that looking at the environment, the approach, and the activities that help the nervous system feel calm and regulated can also provide clues to determine the strengths in sensory processing.

In Chapter 4, you will turn your magnifying glass on yourself to discover your sensory processing abilities! You will learn:

- How you process sensory information
- Which sensory systems you use to learn best
- Which sensory information can be disorganizing for you
- Which sensory information can help you feel calm and relaxed
- How to recognize signs that your body is regulated, calm, and relaxed and when your body is not
- How to communicate what we need to our teacher and other students in a respectful way

Chapter
Four

Self-Discovery

Learning Objectives—
In this chapter, teachers and students will learn:

- The "just right" state
- A sensory journey
- Sensory screening
- Signs of a regulated and disregulated nervous system
- Differences in sensory processing
- A classroom sensory summary
- How to design your sensory space (bedroom and classroom)
- How to design interaction style from a sensory perspective
- How to design a sensory lifestyle

This chapter is full of entertaining activities designed to help all you Sensory Detectives better understand your own nervous system. How do you process sensation? What are your strengths in sensory processing? Let's begin …

Understanding yourself is one of the greatest adventures of all! You have learned a lot about the nervous system and how sensation is processed. You have also learned that a sensory processing disorder can have a big impact on the body's functions, health, emotion, and behavior. Your ability to process sensation can be different at school in comparison to home. It can be different in the morning in comparison to the afternoon. It can also be different in certain subjects in comparison to others.

The "Just Right" State

Dr. Jean Ayres spoke about the "just right" state as the optimum state of function in the nervous system: not so much sensation that we are overwhelmed, not so little sensation that we don't notice, just the right amount of sensation that we can process functionally … that is our aim. Keeping our body in the "just right" state is the state of regulation.

Sensory Detectives, let's learn about YOU! What are your sensory strengths? What are the senses that may be challenging to process? The adventure begins …

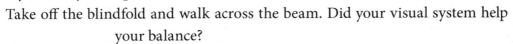

Sensory Journey

How do you respond to different sensations? Let's have some sensory experiences in the classroom. On page 57, you will find a passport. Take this passport to each sensory station and when you have finished the sensory activity, get a stamp on your passport. When your passport is filled, you have completed this sensory journey.

Sensory Station 1 – Vestibular Sensation Station

Put on the blindfold and walk across the balance beam. Can you balance? You are using your vestibular system to balance and your proprioception system to tell you where your body is in space.

Take off the blindfold and walk across the beam. Did your visual system help your balance?

Sensory Station 2 –Auditory Sensation Station

Different items are in plastic containers with lids. The items include:

- Coins
- Water
- Small stones
- Cloth
- Sand
- Rice

Can you tell by moving the plastic containers which objects make which sounds?

Put on a blindfold and have a friend shake a container in front, behind, to the right, to the left, far away, and close to you. Can you use both ears to locate the source of the sound?

Sensory Station 3 – Visual Sensation Station

Play "I spy" with your friend and try to find the object that your friend has challenged you to find. Try to find the object by looking through a paper tube (like the one that holds paper towels) and then try to find it without the tube. Which is easier for you?

Play zoom ball with your partner and watch the ball move toward you and away from you. When the ball comes toward you, do you feel like you may fall?

Put a sticker on the end of a Popsicle stick. Have a friend move it toward your nose and away from your nose starting from 30 inches away and moving in to 15 inches away. When does the sticker get blurry? Can you follow the sticker with your eyes as it goes out and in?

Sensory Station 4 – Tactile Sensation Station

Several items have been placed in a bag. Pull out the item requested using touch alone. Can you guess the items?

- Carrot
- Paper clip
- Rock
- Spoon
- Toilet paper roll

- Cotton ball
- Tennis ball
- Nail file
- Coin
- Pencil

Collect the following items and make sure that each pair of items is the same. Put them in a bag and try to find pairs by using only touch. No peeking! Can you match them?

- Two marbles
- Two ping pong balls
- Two squash balls
- Two balls of aluminum foil
- Two tennis balls

Have a friend draw letters on your back. Can you guess them? Have your friend draw letters on your hand. Can you guess them? Which is easier?

Sensory Station 5 – Gustatory Sensation Station

Put on a blindfold and place an item of food from the tray in your mouth. A friend can pass you the pieces of food on toothpicks. Can you guess what the food items are? They can include:

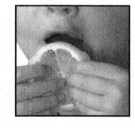

- Piece of banana
- Piece of apple
- Piece of a sour candy
- Chip

- Piece of lemon
- Piece of chocolate
- Piece of bread or muffin

Sensory Station 6 – Olfactory Sensation Station

Put on a blindfold and smell each of the containers. Can you identify what you are smelling? The smells can include:

- Lemon
- Onion or garlic
- Coffee
- Toothpaste

- Maple syrup
- Banana
- Cereal
- Mint

- Oregano
- Cinnamon
- Ginger

Sensory Station 7 – Praxis Station

Write you name backward on the paper in front of you. Did you have to work extra hard to figure out how to form the letters?

Copy three yoga positions:

- Tree
- Eagle
- Warrior 2

Were you able to put your body into these positions?

Sensory Station 8 – Balance and Posture

Start by standing, sit down on the floor, and get up to stand again. Were you able to do the transitions easily?

Sensory Station 9 – Interoception Sensation Station

Describe the changes that happen to your physical body when you feel mad, frustrated, excited, happy, sad, worried, and tired. Demonstrate an emotion physically and have your friend guess what you are feeling.

Sensory Station 10 – Putting It All Together Sensation Station

Stand on the rocker board facing your partner, sing the alphabet song, and throw/catch the beanbag all at the same time. How did you do?

Sensory Passport

			STAMP
1		Vestibular sensation station	
2		Auditory sensation station	
3		Visual sensation station	
4		Tactile sensation station	
5		Taste sensation station	
6		Smell sensation station	
7		Planning sensation station	
8		Balance + Posture sensation station	
9		Interoception sensation station	
10		Putting it all together sensation station	

·Have fun· Learn· Explore· Investigate· stretch·

You did it, Sensory Detective! Way to go!!!

How Can a Sensory Detective Learn about His or Her Own Sensory Processing?

In Chapter 3, we learned that sensory processing assessments can be formal with standardized assessments filled out by your teacher and parents and graded by an occupational therapist, psychologist, or special education teacher. You can also learn about your sensory processing using an informal sensory checklist with two columns, one for home and one for school. Teachers, we'd like you to participate too! We are all in this adventure together.

 Sensory Detectives, sharpen your pencils and find a quiet place to fill out the sensory questionnaire. There are no right or wrong answers.

 Hi, Sensory Detective! Please rate the ability from 1 to 3 that best describes your behavior in the following activities.

1 = never
2 = sometimes
3 = always

The column in the center is for home and the column on the right is for school. This will make it easy to see if you process sensory information differently at home and at school.

The easiest way to determine your sensory strengths and areas of challenge is to see what you like. Generally, what you like is what you can comfortably process. What you don't like may have sensation that is difficult for you to process.

Vestibular Sensation	Home	School
1. Are you afraid on playground equipment?		
2. Are you afraid of climbing up/down stairs?		
3. Would you ever climb a rope ladder?		
4. Do you get sick on elevators or in cars?		
5. Do you like going on carnival rides?		
6. Do you avoid activities that require you to balance?		
7. Do you like to play sports?		
8. Do you like running up/down hills?		
9. Do you lose your place when you are reading?		
10. Do you feel dizzy when you move?		
11. Do you love moving?		
12. Do you have difficulty staying still?		
13. Do you like spinning on the spot?		
14. Do you often rock or move your head?		

What movements do you enjoy?

_____

_____

_____

What movement activities do you like to do?

_____

_____

_____

Touch Sensation	Home	School
1. Do you like to touch wet messy things (like paint)?		
2. Do you like to touch new textures or do you choose to look at them only?		
3. Does some clothing bother you?		
4. Do tags, elastic waistbands, and seams in clothing bother you?		
5. Is it difficult to wear socks or new shoes?		
6. Does it bother you when someone is standing close to you?		
7. Are you bothered by your sweat on hot days?		
8. Is it difficult to eat food that has different textures?		
9. Do you like brushing your teeth?		
10. Do you like brushing your hair?		
11. Do you like touching objects?		
12. Do you have difficulty holding an item for a long time, like a pencil?		
13. Do you like things that vibrate?		
14. Do you like to put objects in your mouth to feel them?		

What kind of touch do you like?

_____

_____

_____

What touch activities do you enjoy?

_____

_____

_____

Proprioception Sensation	Home	School
1. Do you push too hard with your pencil when you write?		
2. Do you often squish things by holding them too tightly?		
3. Do you bump into things often?		
4. Do you talk too loudly?		
5. Do you slam doors shut when you mean to close them quietly?		
6. Is it easy for you to learn how to position your body in new yoga movements?		
7. Do you like rough-and-tumble play?		
8. Do you like squeezing yourself into tight places?		
9. Do you relax when you are hugged or receiving a massage?		

What positions are your favorite positions to sit, stand, and lie down?

_____

_____

_____

What proprioception activities do you enjoy?

_____

_____

_____

Visual Sensation	Home	School
1. Are you uncomfortable in sunlight?		
2. Are you uncomfortable in strong light?		
3. Do you notice changes in lighting?		
4. Do your eyes hurt when you look at a computer or television screen for a long time?		
5. Is it difficult to look at faces?		
6. Is it difficult to look someone in the eye?		
7. Do you like to watch things that spin?		
8. Do you like looking at distant things?		
9. Do you like watching things like a fish tank or lava lamp?		
10. Do you notice visual changes easily (like something being different; your friend with a new haircut or wearing new glasses)?		
11. Do you like looking at things that are complicated (like maps or visual games)?		

What colors and things do you like looking at the most?

_____

_____

_____

What are your favorite visual activities?

_____

_____

_____

Auditory Sensation	**Home**	**School**
1. Do you get frightened or upset by loud sounds (like the recess bell or thunder)?		
2. Do you jump in fright at an unexpected sound (like the PA system)?		
3. Do you sometimes hum or sing to block out sounds?		
4. Do you find some sounds painful (like the vacuum or the hair drier)?		
5. Do you like lots of sound (like a concert or an assembly)?		
6. Do you whisper when you are talking to your friends?		
7. Do you like to turn up the volume on the radio/TV/computer?		
8. Is it difficult to listen to one voice when there is a lot of noise in the environment?		
9. Do people's voices sometimes sound like they are under water?		
10. Do you mix sounds up and think a person says something totally different?		

What sounds and what volumes of sound do you like?

_____

_____

_____

What auditory activities do you enjoy?

_____

_____

_____

Olfactory/Gustatory Sensation	Home	School
1. Do you like to smell strong smells?		
2. Do you like the smells of different foods cooking?		
3. Do you gag when you see or smell certain foods?		
4. Do you like to taste new foods?		
5. Do you like to eat and drink foods that are cold?		
6. Do you like to eat and drink foods that are hot?		
7. Do you like the taste of toothpaste?		
8. Do you like to taste things that are not for eating?		
9. Do you like it when people wear perfume?		
10. Do you like the smell of shampoo/laundry detergent?		
11. Do you enjoy when the seasons change and there are new smells outdoors?		

What are your favorite smells and tastes?

_____

_____

_____

What are your favorite smell and taste activities?

_____

_____

_____

Interoception Sensation	Home	School
1. Do you feel when you are hungry?		
2. Do you feel when you have to use the toilet?		
3. Do you feel when you are thirsty?		
4. Do you feel when you are tired?		
5. Can you feel when you are frustrated?		
6. Can you feel when you are angry?		
7. Can you feel when you are sad?		
8. Can you feel when you are happy?		
9. Can you feel when you are excited?		
10. Can you feel when you are worried?		
11. Can you feel when you are shy?		
12. Can you feel when you are overwhelmed?		
13. Can you feel when you are getting hot and starting to sweat?		
14. Can you feel when you're getting bored and losing attention?		

What are the signs that your body and nervous system use to suggest that you are becoming overwhelmed?

_____

_____

_____

Is it easy for you to read your own body and nervous system signs?

_____

_____

_____

What do you do when your body and nervous system feel overwhelmed and you want to get back to the "just right" state of regulation?

_____

_____

What activities do you like to avoid when you want to get your body and nervous system back to the "just right" state of regulation?

_____

_____

Do you like an adult to help you regulate your nervous system and get back to the "just right" state? Who would this person be at home/school?

_____

_____

How do you want the adult to help your nervous system get back to the "just right" state of regulation?

_____

_____

What would you like the adult to say to help you feel better?

_____

_____

What are the signs that you know your body and your nervous system are back in the "just right" state of regulation?

_____

_____

How long does it usually take to get your body and nervous system back in the "just right" state of regulation? It is faster at home or at school? Why?

_____

_____

Sensory Strengths

 Sensory Detectives, did you discover new information about yourself?

What are your sensory strengths? Which senses can be challenging for you to process? Were there differences between your scores at home and at school? Different environments offer different sensory experiences. When we are in a comfortable environment, it can be easier to process sensation. Also, when an environment is organized, it can be easier to process sensation because we can predict the sensation we will experience.

Make a list of your sensory strengths and the activities you enjoy that contain those sensations:

Sensory Strengths	Activities

Sensory Dysregulation

Make a list of the signs that suggest that your body and nervous system are overwhelmed and what you can do to help regain the "just right" state of regulation. The super savers are activities, people, and environments that help you return to the "just right" state of regulation.

Signs of My Body and Nervous System Being in Dysregulation	Super Savers

Interview Activity

The next activity is an interview activity in which you use the questionnaire and interview one of your friends in the class. Compare your summaries. Do you have similar or different sensory strengths? Do you enjoy similar or different sensory activities? What about your body's and nervous system's signs of dysregulation and super savers? Which strategies are the same? Are some different?

Sensory Detectives, you will find that some people are a lot like you and some people are different. There is no right or wrong answer. This is the way your nervous system works. Understanding how YOU work is very important! Reading your own signs of dysregulation and choosing a strategy that helps you return to the "just right" state is what this curriculum is all about. Your function and occupation as a student, a learner, a teacher, a friend, a helper—all need a regulated nervous system to work.

The nervous system operates in a similar fashion in all of us. We learned the anatomy and the electrical/chemical communication of the nervous system in Chapter 2.

We are all exposed to different experiences, have different families, and form different memories of events. The experiences we have as we develop create differences in our sensory and emotional processing. This is what makes us unique!

Knowing about your sensory strengths and how to read the signs of your body and nervous system when you are overwhelmed helps you regain the "just right" state of regulation. It enables you to stay calm and choose an activity that will help you stay calm.

When you understand the sensory strengths and how to read the signs of your friend's disregulated nervous system, you can support your friend to stay in the "just right" regulated state.

Sometimes we need to add activities and reassurances to maintain or regain our regulated state and sometimes we need to take demands, interaction, and sensation away to help us regain our regulated state. We are all individuals and our own needs can change.

The ability to read our signs and know what people, activities, and sensations we need to regain our "just right" state is the key to regulation.

Putting It All Together

 Sensory Detectives, it may be helpful to put the sensory strengths of the whole class together in chart form. It will be easy see all the sensory needs of the whole class by looking at one chart!

The chart may look something like this:

Summary of Sensory Strengths

Sense	# of Students	Sensory Activities in the Classroom That Offer Sensation
1. Vestibular		
2. Proprioception		
3. Tactile		
4. Auditory		
5. Visual		
6. Olfactory		
7. Gustatory		
8. Interoception		

Information from a chart like this helps you plan your environment, your daily schedule of activities, free time choices, and sensory modifications that students may need so that they can:

1. Stay in the "just right" state of regulation.
2. Optimize function and success as a student.
3. Create a culture of understanding and celebration of diversity.
4. Support each other to succeed in the classroom.

Sensory Detectives know that when the environment meets their sensory needs they can do anything! The sky is the limit!

Designing Your Space

The next activity requires you to combine your research with your imagination. You will create your bedroom space and your classroom space. Some of your ideas will make these places more comfortable for you, but not all of your fabulous ideas will be able to be implemented; you can save them for when your design your own house.

Our environments are extremely important to our ability to regulate the state of our nervous system. Some people like quiet, dark places and love reading. They may create a cool space under their bed with one light source where they can read every day. Some people love sunshine and wind and will make sure that their space has access to the outdoors.

We are all different! Some people do their homework in a quiet space and cannot be disturbed. Other people do their homework with the radio on in the middle of a busy kitchen. There are no right and wrong ways to set up your environment. However, your environment needs sensory experiences that help your nervous system feel "just right."

 Sensory Detectives, time to put your thinking caps on again. These next activities are lots of fun! You need to remember your sensory strengths and the activities you enjoy to perform these next activities. Have fun!

Let's start in your home. Think about your bedroom. Do you have your own or do you share? Things to think about before you start your design include:

Do you like to move (vestibular sense)? How much open space do you need? What pieces of equipment do you need to help you move (e.g., mini trampoline, yoga mat)?

_____

_____

Do you like tight places (proprioception sense)? Is there space under your bed for a tiny place to squeeze into? Do you need pillows, a heavy weighted blanket, or onesies?

_____

_____

Do you have textures in your room that you enjoy touching (tactile sense)? Do you have soft sheets, blankets, stuffed toys, or pjs?

_____

_____

Designing Your Space

Are there sounds that you enjoy in your room (auditory sense)? Do you have a radio/CD player or something that can play your favorite music? Do you have headphones so that you can make your room quieter (especially if you share your room)?

_____

_____

What colors do you like to look at (visual sense)? What color should your walls be?

_____

_____

Do you enjoy looking at a lot of things at the same time or do you like blank walls (visual sense)?

_____

If you share a room with a messy brother or sister and you need an uncluttered organized space (or vice versa), you can hang a curtain down the middle of your room to divide your space visually.

What kind of light do you like (visual sense)? Are you close to a window if you like natural light? Do you like an overhead light or the light from a bedside lamp? Do you like a nightlight?

_____

_____

What smells do you like (olfactory sense)? Is it possible to have those smells in your room (favorite laundry detergent, skin lotions, little bottles of favorite smells, a sachet tucked in your pillow) or no smell at all?

_____

_____

Taste is not a sense we usually experience in a bedroom, but you might enjoy having snacks in your room. If you did want snacks, what would they be (gustatory sense)? What tastes would you like?

_____

_____

Designing Your Space

Do you have the ability to manage the temperature in your room so that you don't get too hot or too cold (interoception sense)? Do you have a place to store water if you're thirsty or snacks if you're hungry (interoception sense)? Do you have a journal in which you can draw or write about how you are feeling (interoception sense)? Do you have timers/alerts/alarms to let you know when you need to get up? Do you have a pet that can help you feel better? Do you have easy access to the bathroom?

_____

_____

_____

_____

_____

_____

Designing Your Space

Design your perfect bedroom based on all the careful considerations you have made.

— your current bedroom —

— your bedroom incorporating sensory ideas —

Designing Your Space

 Well done, Sensory Detectives! You have thoughtfully designed your bedroom based on your sensory needs. Some of you may have had to be flexible, especially if you share a room with a brother or sister. You may want to design the place where you do homework in a similar way so that your environment matches the sensory needs of your nervous system.

Now let's design something larger!

Let's design your classroom. This is a larger space and a bigger job because many people share this space. When the teacher knows the sensory needs of the students, the teacher can build in some cool design features that meet those sensory needs and still enable the classroom to function as a classroom. Your teacher needs to know the sensory needs of the classroom and can use the chart you developed on page 70.

Do you need to move (vestibular sense)? How much open space do you need? What pieces of equipment do you need to help you move (e.g., mini trampoline, rocker board, stretchy bands, yoga mat)?

_____

_____

How many movement breaks do you need? How long should the movement breaks be?

_____

_____

Would you like your desk near the door (so you can access bigger space in the hall) or near the back of the room (so you can access space in the classroom)?

_____

_____

Do you need tight places (proprioception sense)? Is there space under your desk for a tiny place to squeeze into? Is there a tent or a fort in your classroom? Is there a quiet library corner? Do you need stretchy bands? Do you need pillows, a heavy weighted blanket, or a lap snake? Do you need a compression vest? Do you need a vibrating pen? Massager?

_____

_____

_____

Designing Your Space

Do you need textures in your classroom that you enjoy touching (tactile sense)? Do you have tactile bins filled with different tactile adventures? Can you cover you desktop and/or pens with textures you enjoy?

_____

_____

Are there sounds that you enjoy in your classroom (auditory sense)? Do you need a radio/CD/iPod, MP3 player, or something that can play your favorite music? Do you have headphones so that you can make your classroom quieter?

_____

_____

What colors do you need to look at (visual sense)? What color should the area on your desk or around you be?

_____

_____

Do you enjoy looking at a lot of things at the same time or do you like blank walls (visual sense)? Where would you like to put your desk in the classroom? Can you move your desk so that it faces something else?

_____

_____

If you need an uncluttered organized space and your classroom is full of color and objects to look at, you can, for example, put a three-sided cardboard space separator on top of your desk which instantly blocks out competing visual sensation.

Do you need to see your schedule visually? Do you need to see reminders about what you need to do (e.g., reminder to *put up your hand* on a poster on the wall in front of you)?

_____

_____

What kind of light do you need (visual sense)? Are you close to a window if you like natural light? Do you like an overhead light or the light from a lamp? Do you need to wear a baseball cap to block out light?

_____

_____

Designing Your Space

What smells do you need (olfactory sense)? Is it possible to have access to your favorite smells in your classroom (skin lotions, little bottles of favorite smells, a sachet tucked in your desk, smelly pencils/markers/crayons)? Do you like no smell at all?

_____

_____

Which snacks would you need (gustatory sense)? What tastes would you like? Would you need water? What about water flavored with lemon or something else?

_____

_____

Can you manage the temperature in your classroom so that you don't get too hot or too cold (interoception sense)? Do you need to feel moving air and have a fan?

_____

Do you have a place to store water if you're thirsty or snacks if you're hungry (interoception sense)?

_____

Do you need a journal in which you can draw or write about how you are feeling (interoception sense)?

_____

Do you need a schedule/timer/alerts/alarms to let you know when you need to do things or finish up?

_____

Do you need a classroom pet or a stuffed toy to help you feel calm and organized (interoception sense)?

_____

Do you have easy access to the bathroom and do you need a washroom schedule (interoception sense)?

_____

Designing Your Space

Design your perfect classroom based on all the careful considerations you have made.

— your current classroom —

— your classroom incorporating sensory ideas —

Designing the Way People Interact with You

Sensory Detectives, great job designing your space with your sensory needs in mind. Next we are going to design interaction with others with your sensory needs in mind. When the nervous system is calm, we are able to listen and learn better, do our schoolwork better, interact with others better, and regulate our emotions and behavior better. We interact with other people throughout the day. Let's design an interaction style that works for YOU.

Activity	True	False
1. When I talk with people, I like to stay still.		
2. When I talk with people, I like to stand and move.		
3. I like people to look at me directly.		
4. I like people to face me but not look directly at me.		
5. I like people to sing or use rhythm when giving instructions.		
6. I like people to speak quietly.		
7. I like people to speak in a loud voice.		
8. I like people to speak slowly.		
9. I like people to stand close to me.		
10. I like people to stand a little distance away - no touching.		
11. I like people to have a nice smell.		
12. I like people to have no smell.		
13. I like people to have lots of facial expressions.		
14. I like people to have a neutral face.		

Sensory Detectives, you can tell people how you want them to interact with you and give you direction. You can explain that this will help you listen and learn. This process is called self-advocacy and it is the ability to state what you need to be able to function at your best.

Designing the Way People Interact with You

Teachers have the very important task of preparing children for life! Teachers give children the tools they need to continue their education and establish their career. Self-advocacy is a skill that will empower students throughout their life. When students know their sensory needs and can meet those needs through sensory activities to stay regulated, they can manage their own behavior in the classroom. When students regulate their own behavior, teachers will have more time to teach.

We have designed environments and interaction styles that match your sensory strengths. We can also design the way we do activities, the order of activities, and the frequency and duration of activities to match our sensory strengths and enable our nervous system to stay calm and regulated.

A Sensory Lifestyle

Sensory diet is a term used to describe a list of sensory activities that are placed within the schedule of the day. The goal of a sensory diet is to provide the nervous system with the sensation it needs to maintain a calm and regulated state. Dr. Lucy Miller, PhD OTR, suggested that we call the infusion of sensory activities into our schedule a sensory lifestyle. Knowledge about our own sensory strengths and needs enables us to plan our own sensory lifestyles so that we can maintain our own regulated state.

Sensory Detectives, do you remember when you summarized your sensory strengths and the activities you like that contain those sensations? Go back and refer to that summary for the next activity.

Lise Faulise, OTR, suggested that we consider sensory activities like a bank account. We put calm organized sensation into our nervous system through sensory activities so that we can stay calm and organized during activities that may not match our nervous system. More difficult days require more sensory "deposits" so that we can have more "withdrawals" of regulation.

Sensory Detectives, we will do one more activity before moving on to Chapter 5. We will design a school day that has sensory activities spread throughout the day. We'll begin with an example and then you will design your own day.

Marc's muscle tone, the "readiness of his muscles to perform work," seemed to be at the low end of the normal range. Marc loved movement and deep-pressure activities. These activities helped him know the position of his body in space and generate muscle tone to sit and maintain an upright posture. Here is Marc's sensory lifestyle schedule:

Child's Name:	*Marc*
Date:	*December 2016*
Sensory strengths:	*Visual, auditory, tactile sensation*
Sensory needs:	*Vestibular and proprioception sensation*
Goals:	*Increase postural stamina, decrease Marc leaning on other students, increase success in learning at school.*
Signs of Marc in a regulated state:	*Smiling, interested, involved, pretty still, voice is quiet, moves slowly.*
Signs of Marc in a dysregulated state:	*Doesn't want to participate, decreased eye contact, flopping body on the floor, loud voice.*

Time	Activity
8:00 AM	*Put on compression vest or long johns under clothing to go to school. Wear a knapsack. Eat a breakfast with lots of crunchy foods.*
8:15 AM	*Bus ride—Marc sits at the back of the bus where the bumps are highest.*
8:45 AM	*Arrival—Marc hangs up his coat and puts away his lunch. He pulls the heavy wagon with the mats for circle and places them on the carpet.*
9:00 AM	*Morning circle—Marc sits in a howda seat (www.howda.com) and rocks back and forth.*
9:20 AM	*Marc helps the teacher pick up the mats and pulls the heavy wagon to the back of the classroom.*
9:30 AM	*Reading—Marc sits in the rocking chair for reading.*
10:30 AM	*Writing—Marc sits on his mambo seat or stands to work on the easel. He warms his hands up with a vibrating pen before he starts his writing.*
10:45 AM	*Recess—Marc gets ready five minutes before the rest of his class to accommodate his balance needs in a busy cubby area. Marc takes a weighted ball out for recess. He loves playing with it and it moves somewhat slowly so Marc is able to get it back without too much running after it.*
11:15 AM	*Gym—Marc can become disorganized in such a large space. Movement activities prior to gym are very helpful. Marc pushes and holds the heavy fire doors for his classmates on the way to the gym.*
12:00 PM	*Lunch—Marc goes to get his lunch two minutes before his class. He eats at the end of a lunch table on a mambo or hokki seat. Mom packs him lots of crunchy foods.*
12:20 PM	*Lunch recess—Before going out for recess, Marc helps the janitor by lifting the chairs to put them on the tables. Then he goes out for recess with his weighted ball.*
1:00 PM	*Arts and crafts—Marc prefers standing so he can stand at his desk or work at the easel. Listening to music is one of Marc's favorite activities during art.*
1:45 PM	*Science—Marc can use his vibrating pen to warm up his hands and arms before writing or pouring liquids.*
2:15 PM	*Afternoon recess—Marc is able to take the scooter out for recess and loves riding it on the bumpy schoolyard surface.*
2:30 PM	*Social studies—Marc hands out the papers to his classmates. He sits on his mambo seat.*
3:00 PM	*Home time! Marc prepares five minutes early.*

Can You Create Your Sensory Lifestyle?

Child's Name:

Date:

Sensory strengths:

Sensory needs:

Goals:

Signs of Marc in a regulated state:

Signs of Marc in a dysregulated state:

List activities that you can do during the day to keep your nervous system calm and alert.

8:00 AM

8:15 AM

8:45 AM

9:00 AM

9:20 AM

9:30 AM

10:30 AM

10:45 AM

11:15 AM

12:00 PM

12:20 PM

1:00 PM

1:45 PM

2:15 PM

2:30 PM

3:00 PM

Chapter Five

Identifying Sensory Processing Disorders

Learning Objectives—
In this chapter, teachers and students will learn:

- How sensory processing support attention, executive functions, and regulation
- About stressors - physical, sensory, and social-emotional
- About Interoception
- Sensory processing disorders

So far, we have seen that sensory processing is a complex process that occurs constantly—whether we're awake or asleep! Our brain processes and organizes information from both our bodies and the world around us to make it meaningful to us. We saw in Chapter 3 what can happen when sensory information is not organized and labeled accurately; it can affect all the activities and tasks we perform in our day. In Chapter 4, we learned that all of us have both strengths and challenges in sensory processing. Our stress level, our emotions and feelings, and our current environment can all affect our sensory processing.

We can imagine sensory processing as the balancing act of riding a teeter-totter. We all strive to get through our day as efficiently and effortlessly as possible. We need to understand where our body is in space, use feedback from our tactile sense, use appropriate muscle force (our proprioception system), and motor plan all the steps to get dressed in the morning. If extra stressors such as a lack of sleep are present, the processing of sensation and the planning of dressing may be difficult.

When the school bell rings to signal the end of lunch, we need to be able to follow our friends, line up, and go back to class. If we slept in that morning, arrived late to school, and found that we had a substitute teacher and a change in the schedule for the day, our nervous system may feel disregulated. We may jump from the sudden shrill sound of the bell and overreact because we were not expecting it. Our body may be stressed because of our morning and may not process the sudden sound and respond appropriately.

We can use the teeter-totter analogy to visualize the balancing act of the environmental demand and our ability to process sensation as we try our best to stay alert and focused to play and learn throughout the day. We work to screen out background noise like a ticking clock to focus on the teacher's voice. We can inhibit, or avoid focusing on, the feeling of our clothing on our body and focus on the feeling of the paintbrush in our hand as we paint a picture in art class.

If we become tired and lose our focus, we may begin to fidget and move in our chair. Movement can help increase our arousal and help us pay attention and focus. The brain can be more alert in movement and in standing as we increase the amount of vestibular information. Remember that the vestibular sense is our master sense and can have a big effect on our attention and arousal (staying in the "ready" state). Movement also affects the endolymph (specialized fluid) in the structures of our inner ear. We can detect linear movement when the endolymph moves in the utricle and saccule and we can detect rotational movement when the endolymph moves in the semi-circular canals. It is amazing! We are constantly assessing our position in space because our body needs to continually balance and shift. This constant maintenance of balance actually helps us maintain our arousal levels, our attention, and our focus. It's a really neat side effect of movement.

Standing also makes it easier for us to breathe efficiently by giving our diaphragm, the muscle of breathing, more space to move. When our diaphragm moves better, we can take in more air and the more air we take in, the more oxygen we have available to energize our blood and feed our muscles.

The ability to attend to the state of our body and nervous system, choose a strategy to maintain our calm, alert state, and match our response to the demand of our environment on an ongoing basis is called self-regulation. When we can maintain our calm alert state in response to our sensory environment, it is called sensory modulation. In a nutshell, sensory modulation is the ability to stay in tune with ourselves, and our environment, and if we're not in tune we know what to do to regain that state. That is what this curriculum is all about.

Let's review … our ability to balance or regulate sensory input from our bodies and the environment helps us keep our bodies feeling organized and alert. When our nervous system is in the "just right" or "ready" state, we can decide which sensory information is important at that moment and attend to it and which sensory information is not important. Information that we can ignore doesn't give us new information and doesn't contribute to our ability to perform our present task; it is a part of the background. When we cannot decide what sensory information to pay attention to, all sensation enters our nervous system tagged with the same level of importance, which can be overwhelming to our nervous system, like a big wave of sensation. In contrast, we can sometimes be underaroused and have difficulty noticing sensory input in the first place. When we are underaroused, we benefit from more sensory input of the same kind. The ability to modulate sensation helps us maintain our ready state and arousal levels. Optimum arousal helps us decide what we need to focus on and attend to. It's like the beam of a flashlight that shines on one object and makes it easier to see in contrast to the darker surrounding. An optimal level of arousal is necessary for:

- Attention
- Impulse control
- Emotional regulation
- Executive functions (working memory, reasoning, cognitive flexibility, considering multiple aspects of a task at once, adjusting attention in response to a new goal or environment, problem solving, planning and execution of a motor response)

Success at our tasks helps us develop a sense of ourselves. It enables the development of our character and personality!

Stress is an interesting phenomenon. We need a low level of stress to motivate us to complete a project by the due date. We need it to pay attention to what our friend is saying so that we can participate in the conversation. It is the feeling that something is "not quite right" in our body; we need to eat or we need to go to the washroom.

When these stress levels are too high, we can experience what we often call STRESS! This is an underlying agitation that can interfere with our body's rhythms, our processing, and our function.

Here are some of the stressors we can experience that can interfere with our sensory regulation:

Stressors that affect our physical body:
- Lack of or disturbed sleep
- Sickness
- Allergies
- Hunger or thirst (even something stuck between our teeth!)
- Pain
- Constipation
- Weather changes—headaches, migraines
- Chair/desk heights affecting posture
- Breathing
- Temperature

Sensory stressors:
- Lighting
- Background noise
- Clothing material or fit
- Environment (space, clutter, position in the classroom)
- Smells like cooking smells or perfumes
- Limited movement opportunities
- Delays in sensory processing

Socio-emotional stressors:

- Family dynamics
- Bullying
- Social difficulties
- Feelings of isolation/exclusion
- Anxiety about fitting in and being a part of the group
- Feelings of competence

Organization:
- Changes in teaching staff
- Friend being absent
- Changes in the schedule (e.g., short day)
- Changes in desk/layout of the classroom
- Changes in the drop-off/pick-up
- Understanding of expectations

Other:
- Understanding of instructions—auditory processing, visual processing
- Difficulty with executive functions

We must become "detectives" when trying to search for clues to understand the behaviors that we and others demonstrate in class that may reflect challenges in sensory processing. Formal assessments by occupational therapists in combination with observations of sensory strengths and challenges in different environments, with different people and during different tasks, are strongly suggested. When evaluating these behaviors, we can take into account what happens before, during, and after the person's behavior. We can also consider feedback from parents through communication sheets and parent/teacher meetings.

To be accurate in determining the underlying reasons for behaviors, we need to pull in all approaches; no one discipline has all the answers. A sensory lens is ONE lens we use in our detective work. In our clinic, we always tell parents … we may know about sensory processing, but you know your child better than we do. The parent and teacher have wonderful knowledge and together can perform the detective work to help get the student who may be having challenges with sensory processing back on track to success!

Many assessments can be used to help determine the sensory processing ability of a student (sensory profile, sensory processing measure, sensory skills inventory, and sensory checklists). These assessments were introduced in Chapter 3. Assessments are a valuable tool to determine underlying sensory processing difficulties. They often support what we observe. Another often overlooked tool for determining strategies to support students is to ask the teacher and parent about what IS working. What are the times, subjects, activities, and strategies that are successful? Approaching challenging behavior from a positive perspective can help shed light on the strengths and interests that the child is already using to succeed.

Dr. Lucy Miller developed a taxonomy or classification system to describe the types of sensory processing disorders. Let's review these subtypes of SPD.

The first subtype is sensory modulation disorder. This is a disorder in the ability to respond or adjust functionally to a sensation. Children can over respond (SOR, sensory over responsiveness), which is described under the hypersensitive behaviors in the chart below. Children can under-respond (SUR, sensory under responsiveness), which is described under the hyposensitive behaviors in the chart below. Children can also be described as sensory seekers or sensory cravers (SCs). These children seek out sensations without reaching satiation. They appear to be thrill seekers, always on the lookout for more sensation.

The second subtype of Dr. Miller's taxonomy is sensory discrimination disorder (SDD). In this subtype, children have difficulty attaching the correct meaning to the sensation they process. They can have difficulty determining the differences between intensities of the same sensation and can even mix up sensations! Behaviors that suggest SDD are listed below.

Sensory-based movement disorder (SBMD) is the third subtype of SPD in Dr. Miller's taxonomy. In this subtype, children can have difficulty adjusting their posture and balance to meet the demands of the environment or they can have dyspraxia. Dyspraxia is the inability to plan a response or sequence the steps of a response.

All subtypes of SPD can make the world a confusing and frustrating place. Difficulty responding accurately to sensation can have a negative effect on function, success, confidence, and self-esteem.

Teachers, here are some behaviors you may observe that can indicate challenges students have with sensory processing:

Sensory Modulation Disorder

Vestibular

Hyper-sensitive:
- Fearful of movement
- Afraid of moving in new positions, especially with feet off the ground
- Avoids playground equipment
- Easily becomes carsick
- Avoids physical activity and prefers sedentary activities
- Challenges with visual tracking
- Dislikes stops/starts or changing directions—such as the school bus stopping at a red light and then turning the corner

Hypo-sensitive:
- Seeks movement input like rocking chair, jumping, running, swinging, car rides, spinning in swing, or chair with wheels, etc.
- Difficulty standing or sitting still
- Challenges with movement
- May lack physical and emotional security
- Seems to lack sense of danger related to heights or movement

- Doesn't seem to get dizzy
- May frequently rock when trying to stay still

Olfactory

Hyper-sensitive:
- Avoids some smells
- Gags or coughs at the sight or smell of certain foods
- May notice smells that others do not
- May avoid people or places because of smell
- May cover their nose with their hand or shirt
- Eyes watering in response to a smell
- May turn their head away or make a funny face

Hypo-sensitive:
- Seeks out strong smells
- Smears feces (this could also be a child who is hypersensitive to smell and using a strong smell to block out other smells)
- Eats non-edible foods
- Does not seem to respond to noxious smells

Tactile

Hyper-sensitive:
- Challenges with clothes made out of certain materials, tags, or seams
- Bothered by being touched unexpectedly or if someone is too close
- Avoids messy play or messy snacks—e.g. glue on hands, getting wet—and may want to wash or wipe their hands frequently
- Meltdowns when hair is brushed or during visits to the hair dresser
- Challenges lining up or during circle time
- May have challenges being touched if they cannot see the person or object touching them
- May have difficulty with changes in the temperature
- May have difficulty changing clothing when seasons change
- May have difficulty tolerating stiff formal clothing
- May demonstrate "lip splays" to certain foods by pulling their lips back and cleaning the spoon with their teeth and not their lips

- "Finger splaying"—may have their fingers wide apart while touching certain foods or materials to touch the object as little as possible
- May be really efficient at using tools while eating to avoid touching the foods themselves (or similar with crafts)
- Grimacing

Hypo-sensitive:
- May not notice being touched
- May not seem to respond appropriately to objects that are too hot or too cold
- May not notice changes in temperature and dress inappropriately for the weather
- Always touching things
- Constantly mouths objects
- Unaware of food on their face
- May not notice when part of their body gets dirty or wet
- Tends to use their mouth and hands to learn about new toys and objects
- May swallow foods whole or barely chewed as they are not getting adequate feedback from the tactile and proprioceptive systems

Proprioceptive

Hyper-sensitive:
- May seem defensive to hugs
- May avoid activities that involve moving and stretching their body
- Often have a rigid posture
- May avoid physical activities that involve running, jumping, crashing, etc.

Hypo-sensitive:
- Often bump into people or objects in the environment—seems to have poor body awareness
- Frequently fall out of chairs
- Challenges staying in one place and like to move frequently
- May have a "floppy" posture
- Frequently drops books, pencils, cups, etc.
- Tires easily
- Challenges judging force, such as too hard or too light High 5s
- Pressing too hard while writing with a pencil
- Seeks out rough-housing activities

- Loves firm massages
- Loves chewing on things to stay focused (e.g., shirt, pencil)—though this strategy can also be related to other underlying vision and posture challenges

Visual

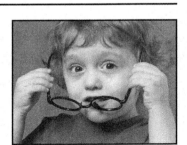

Hyper-sensitive:
- Squinting, repeated eye blinking, eye watering or rubbing
- Challenges with bright lights
- May have challenges with flashing or moving lights
- May often rub their eyes
- Could have challenges with changes to lighting in the classroom
- May have difficulty when the sun changes its position during the change in seasons
- May avoid looking directly at a person or object
- Avoid eye contact
- Do not look directly at objects using central, focal vision
- Use peripheral vision

Hypo-sensitive:
- Like to watch falling objects or spinning objects
- Focus on shadows
- Difficulty staying between the lines while writing
- May miss facial expressions

Other/functional signs of visual difficulty that suggest a visit to a behavioral optometrist:
- Frequently loses their place while reading
- Difficulty with convergence (using two eyes together)
- Difficulty tracking (following a moving object with the eyes)
- May see biting on objects
- Holding and waving fingers up near eyes
- Experiences headaches, dizziness, nausea, or fatigue easily after reading
- Head tilting, closing, or blocking one eye when focusing
- Difficulty following moving objects
- Challenges distinguishing "b" vs. "d"
- May miss important non-verbal communication
- Challenges discriminating shapes

- Difficulty making sense of facial expressions and gestures
- May see all the details but miss the whole picture
- Challenges with depth perception, such as going down stairs or stepping down from a curb

Auditory

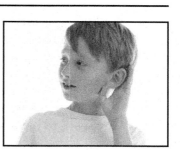

Hyper-sensitive:
- Challenges working in environment with many background sounds
- Upset when vacuum or blow dryer is on
- May hum or sing to screen out background noise or speak in a loud voice
- Frequently covers ears (may include during meals)
- May avoid environments or situations where there will be a lot of noise, like ceremonies in the gym or dances
- May not tolerate others singing around them
- Could have challenges moving between quieter and louder environments
- Repeated eye blinking suggesting stress
- May startle in response to noise

Hypo-sensitive:
- May seek out loud music or sounds
- May hum often

Central auditory processing challenges that may suggest a visit to an audiologist or a speech language pathologist:
- Difficulty responding when name called
- Challenges telling the difference between similar words
- Challenges with timing and sequencing of movements
- Lack of orientation to loud noises
- Difficulty hearing one voice in a loud environment
- Difficulty determining direction of sound
- Difficulty with comprehension

Gustatory

Hyper-sensitive:
- Cannot tolerate certain tastes of food

- Food must be prepared exactly the same each time
- May not be able to tolerate mixing different foods and textures
- Difficulty trying new foods—appears to be a very picky eater
- Gagging, vomiting to tastes, grimacing. or lip splaying (pulling lips away to avoid touching foods on utensil), shuddering in response to foods
- Can become anxious around foods

Hypo-sensitive:
- Unable to tell what is being eaten without looking
- May seem to be able to eat anything
- May have challenges detecting food that is in or around their mouth; may lose food in their mouth
- May pocket food in their mouth (in their cheeks)

Interoception

Hyper-sensitive:
- Use a washroom frequently to avoid painful bowel and bladder sensations
- Avoid using a washroom as the process of elimination can be painful
- May over-eat to avoid the feeling of hunger, which may seem painful
- May get upset by an increase in body temperature
- May be very sensitive to experiencing the response of the body to emotions

Hypo-sensitive:
- Challenges interpreting own body signals—e.g., challenges knowing just how hungry they are; only feel light need to go to washroom when it really is an emergency; challenge knowing if they feel better or worse; difficulty gauging if they are warm or cold, etc.
- Slow to potty-train
- A pounding heart or quick breathing may feel good and then be sought out
- Could have decreased pain responses

Sensory Craving or Seeking

The third subtype of sensory modulation disorder is sensory craving. With this subtype, people seem to actively seek out or crave sensory input and to have an insatiable desire no matter how much input they receive. For instance, a student may be constantly moving, crashing, spinning in circles, or touching things.

Other observations you may notice with a person who tends to be a "sensory seeker" include:
- Challenges with taking turns in a conversation
- May frequently seek control in a situation
- May have difficulty calming down
- May appear overly affectionate physically
- May prefer strong or complex flavors/tastes
- May be constantly in motion or frequently climbing/crashing
- May grind their teeth (although this can be related to anxiety and visual, auditory, or balance challenges as well)
- Could overstuff food into their mouth, which activates the proprioceptive and tactile systems

Sensory Discrimination

People with SDD have difficulty interpreting qualities of sensory stimuli and are unable to perceive similarities and differences among stimuli. They can perceive that stimuli are present and can regulate their response to stimuli but cannot tell precisely what or where the stimulus is (http://spdfoundation.net/pdf/Miller_Anzalone.pdf).

Vestibular
- Seem to have difficulty making sense of input received by moving the body through space or changing the position of your head
- Challenges figuring out their head or body position
- Difficulty knowing what position they are in without looking at their body or in a mirror
- May be quite clumsy
- May fall out of chairs or bump into people or desks
- Seems to have challenges moving on uneven surfaces
- Difficulty maintaining balance when eyes are closed or feet are close together

Olfactory
- Challenges making sense of input that is smelled
- Difficulty telling where a smell is coming from

- May not be able to detect the smell, for example, of something burning
- Challenges telling the difference between two smells

Tactile

- Difficulty making sense of input detected by the skin
- Difficulty knowing what they are holding without looking
- Challenges knowing where on their body they are being touched
- Difficulty describing an object by touch alone (without looking at it)
- Tendency to rely a lot on vision rather than touch to explore the environment
- Unaware of food or drool on face
- May overstuff mouth when eating

Proprioceptive

- Challenges making sense of input detected by the muscles and joints
- Challenges grading how much pressure to exert (e.g., writing with a pencil with too much or too little pressure)
- May frequently rip or tear the page when erasing
- May slam doors or not use enough force to close them
- May exaggerate movements of the arms and legs
- Challenges moving with eyes closed

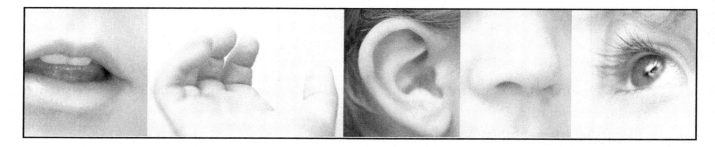

Visual

- May have difficulty interpreting visual information
- May have learning or language disability
- May mistake similar letters like "b" and "d" or "p" and "q"
- Challenges telling the difference between different colors and shapes
- Difficulty figuring out what an object is if part of it is hidden
- Challenges in following a map
- Driving may be tricky, especially parking and merging with traffic
- May have challenges with depth perception

- Difficulty knowing which visuals to attend to in a given room or space
- May confuse left and right
- May have messy writing and drawing
- May have difficulty interpreting facial expressions

Auditory
- May have difficulty interpreting characteristics of auditory information
- May have learning or language disability
- Challenges determining where a sound is coming from or who is speaking to them
- Mistake similar sounds like "cars" and "cards"
- Challenges following instructions that have many steps
- May have difficulty interpreting tone of voice

Gustatory
- May have difficulty interpreting characteristics of taste sensations
- Challenges telling the difference between different tastes
- Difficulty knowing when a food or drink is fresh

Interoception
- Challenges knowing if they need to use the washroom
- Difficulty telling the difference between feeling hungry and full
- Difficulty telling the difference between feeling thirsty and not
- Challenges feeling how fast their heart is beating
- Challenges feeling how fast they are breathing

Resource: http://spdlife.org/symptoms/sensory-discrimination.html and http://spdstar.org/what-is-spd

Sensory-Based Motor Disorder: Posture (the third subtype of SPD)
- May avoid physical activity as quick shifts in posture are challenging
- May prefer sedentary activities
- May have challenges with balance
- May move inefficiently and have poor body awareness
- Makes slow, cautious movements
- Have difficulty moving on an uneven surface (e.g., bumpy ground)
- May need to concentrate to maintain a stable posture or during simple actions like stepping on/off a curb or stepping onto an escalator

- Tends to compensate for their challenges with stability and body control by increasing their "base of support," such as sitting in a "w-sit" position or standing with legs wide apart
- May have poor self-esteem and confidence secondary to difficulties with movement
- May have challenges with bilateral coordination or using both sides of the body at the same time—e.g., stabilizing the page with one hand while writing with the other or stabilizing on one foot while kicking a ball with the other
- Gets tired easily (low endurance)
- May lean on their neighbor at the next desk or at circle time
- May lean on their arm while working at the desk or have their whole upper body resting on the desk itself

Dyspraxia
- Can make clumsy, awkward movements
- Seems disorganized and may make others around them feel disorganized
- May move quickly between tasks
- May have difficulty getting around in a new environment
- Challenges with body awareness
- Challenges sequencing movements in an obstacle course or dance
- Tends to use a toy in the exact same way each time or play a game in the same manner
- Prefers to watch someone else try a new activity first before trying themselves
- Challenges with games and tasks that require imitation—like Simon Says or action songs
- May seem non-compliant when asked to complete structured motor activities
- May not seem interested in a new activity
- Challenges with fine motor skills such as handwriting, buttons, zippers, eating with a fork and knife, tying shoelaces
- Difficulty getting dressed
- Putting on clothes independently
- Determining the order in which to put on clothes
- Putting clothing on in the correct orientation (e.g., putting shirt on backward or shoes on the wrong feet)
- Difficulty modulating voice volume

Observations from Challenges with Processing from One or More Sensory Systems When the World Becomes an Unpredictable Place
- Challenges with transitions between activities
- Constantly seeks out control—e.g., only eating the same brand of chicken nuggets, creating rituals, need for routine, etc.

- Challenges with handwriting
- Challenges with sports
- Increased anxiety
- Increased distractibility
- Highly distressed by changes in the environment
- Overall either very high or very low arousal levels and difficulty attaining and maintaining a regulated arousal level
- May see stereotypic behaviors such as self-stimulation (e.g., hand-flapping, rocking, spinning self or objects, moving objects close to and away from eyes, mouthing or eating non-edible objects) or self-abuse
- Changes in mood
- Increased aggression
- Challenges in crowded places
- Avoiding social situations, such as birthday parties, play dates, etc.
- Socially inappropriate behaviors
- Communication influenced by oral-motor planning affecting speech as well as using alternative ways to communicate (sign language, augmentative communication)

Resource: http://spdlife.org/symptoms

A Note to Teachers about the Sensory Craving or Seeking Subtype of SPD

Individuals with this pattern actively seek or crave sensory stimulation and seem to have an almost insatiable desire for sensory input. They tend to be constantly moving, crashing, bumping, and/or jumping. They may "need" to touch everything and be overly affectionate; not understanding what is "their space" vs. "others' space." Sensory seekers are often thought to have attention deficit hyperactivity disorder (ADHD) or attention deficit disorder (ADD). Many teachers that we consult have asked about the similarity between these diagnoses.

Miller, Nielsen, and Schoen published a study in 2012 in the article "Attention deficit hyperactivity disorder and sensory modulation disorder: A comparison of behavior and physiology." This study speaks to the challenges we can encounter in those individuals with ADHD versus sensory modulation disorder, in particular the sensory craving subtype. These researchers assessed children with ADHD, sensory modulation disorder, and dual diagnoses. They found that all the children had significantly more sensory, attention, activity, impulsivity, and emotional challenges than typical children (Miller, Nielsen, & Schoen, 2012). However, they also found unique characteristics for each group. For example, children with ADHD showed greater inattention than children with sensory modulation disorder. The group of children with dual diagnoses had more sensory-related behaviors than the children ADHD and they also had more attention challenges than the children with sensory modulation disorder. Finally, the group of children with a diagnosis of sensory modulation disorder had more sensory issues, somatic complaints, anxiety/depression, and challenges adapting than children with ADHD.

Furthermore, the children with a diagnosis of sensory modulation disorder had greater physiological/electrodermal reactivity (EDR) to sensory stimulation than children with ADHD and typical controls. Our skin conducts electricity because of eccrine sweat gland activity, which is innervated by the sympathetic nervous system—that part of the nervous system responsible for our fight, flight, and fright reactions. EDR measures electrical changes in the skin as a measure of how much individuals respond to sensory stimuli and can be used as a marker of sympathetic nervous system activity. As a result, these researchers concluded that ADHD and sensory modulation disorder are distinct diagnoses even though they may appear similar (Miller, Nielsen, & Schoen, 2012).

Interoception

We often focus on the senses that give us information about the outside world. However, interoception is becoming more of a focus in our efforts to understand regulation and behavior. The interoception sense gives us information about our internal body. It provides information about:

- Pain
- Body temperature
- Hunger
- Thirst
- Heart rate
- Breathing rate
- Muscle tension
- The need to use the washroom
- Sleepiness
- Sexual arousal
- Itching and more

("Interoception: The eighth sensory system" by Kelly Mahler, p. 1)

These sensations are detected by receptors within the body tissues such as muscle, skin, and internal organs. The insula, a part of the limbic center, or emotional center, in the cortex, receives most of the information regarding interoception from the body. It interprets the messages as either body states, such as hunger or pain, or emotional states, such as excitement or fear (Mahler, p. 7). Our brain then decides how to react, with the goal of reaching homeostasis, or our optimal internal balance that requires the least amount of energy (Mahler, p. 10). This whole process sometimes takes place automatically without any effort on our part; for example, when we feel nervous from an unusual sound, our body reacts in fight, flight, or fright with reactions such as increased heart rate, pupil dilation, and decreased digestion.

At other times, this process may direct us to take action; we may get a drink of water if we are feeling thirsty or ask for help if feeling frustrated on an assignment. The ability to detect these sensations through our interoception system is actually the foundation for self-regulation, since without the awareness of our internal states, it would be impossible to develop efficient self-regulation skills (Mahler, p. 15).

What is also incredibly important to consider is that the interoception forms the foundation for how we view or feel emotions (Mahler, p. 2). If you are presenting in front of the class, you may feel your heart beating faster and your muscles tighten, and you may have difficulty catching your breath. In fact, some leading theories on emotions suggest that emotions are based directly on our body's internal signals (Mahler, p. 17). Neuroscience research has also found that the same part of the brain mentioned above, the insula, is activated both during processing of our internal sensation and during tasks that elicit our emotions (Mahler, p. 17). Research has also found that that our ability to accurately detect and process our internal body sensations enables us to differentiate between emotions (Mahler, p. 18). In other words, having a good sense of interoception contributes to strong emotional awareness, and this in turn leads to improved ability in:

- Controlling one's own emotions
- Flexible thinking
- Access to more and appropriate coping skills
- Improved ability to read other peoples' emotions
- Empathy toward others

(Mahler, pp. 18-19)

Efficient emotional regulation requires us to:

Therefore, if you don't have good interoceptive awareness, you have less information about your current emotions and consequently it is more difficult to react appropriately.

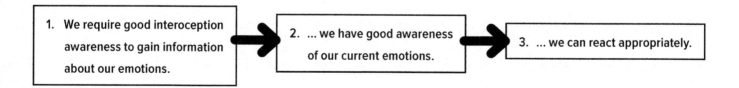

Ideas for How to Promote Interoceptive Awareness

- You can include adaptations where appropriate—such as mirror checks for injuries, alerts on smartphone for washroom or mealtime breaks, weather notifications on phone to check how to dress appropriately before leaving in the morning.
- Some individuals need help tying together body signals with their body state or emotion. (When you use a loud volume and high-pitched voice, it can mean that you are feeling excited.)
- Body scans, similar to those used in mindfulness meditation, can be helpful.
- Visual supports may be helpful for an individual.
- Social stories/video stories may also be useful.
- Only after a person has developed some interoceptive awareness can he or she work on self-regulation by problem solving what can be done when experiencing different emotions or body states, such as when I feel pain in my stomach I can try deep breathing to relax or when I am nervous I can try to think of things that make me happy.

(Mahler, pp. 70-71)

Resource: Mahler, K. (2016). *Interoception—The Eighth Sensory System: Practical Solutions for Improving Self-Regulation, Self-Awareness and Social Understanding in Individuals with Autism Spectrum and Related Disorders.* Lenaxa, Kansas: AAPC Publishing.

Chapter Six

How Can We Support People with Sensory Processing Disorders?

Learning Objectives—
In this chapter, teachers and students will learn:

- Ideas to build a sensory classroom
- Environmental ideas to support self-regulation, executive functions, praxis and body awareness in the classroom
- Sensory strategies to incorporate throughout the school day
- Strategies for a sensory approach
- General regulation strategies
- Co-regulation strategies
- Calming strategies from other disciplines that compliment sensory strategies

What Can We Do to Support People with SPD?

Consider a classroom full of colors, bright lights, and noises. It is energizing for some of us and overwhelming for others. Matching the sensory environment with our sensory strengths and challenges can really support regulation and function.

Teachers, here are some environmental ideas to try for students. Match the environmental strategy to the sensory needs of your students. Try an idea and monitor it to ensure that it is helping the student function more successfully. If the idea doesn't change the student's function, try to determine why and then try another idea. This is a process and students appreciate your attempts to understand and support them in the classroom. You are not on your own. Consult with parents and professionals to help you make choices for your classroom.

General Ideas for a Sensory Classroom
- Have access to fidget bins in the classroom or items within the students' desks.
- Post cards or signs with ideas for movement breaks.
- Have equipment for movement in the classroom for students to access.
- Have sensory bins accessible.
- Have a water station.
- Engage students in tasks of helping (handing out papers, carrying books, delivering items, cleaning the board, delivering the milk).
- Have a listening station with headphones in the classroom.
- Have a quiet place, like a tent, with soft pillows.
- Have a study carrel.
- Use visuals for schedules.
- Minimize visual clutter.

Overall Environmental Ideas to Help with Self-Regulation

Visual:
- Place the student in a spot in the classroom where he/she can see and hear well to help promote learning.
- Have visual reminders within view that suggest more functional behaviors.
- Provide access to a visual schedule to help students predict what will be needed to prepare for in the day ahead and to help with transitions.
- Provide structure and predictability in the day and provide warning if the schedule changes.

Auditory:
- Try background music for the entire class or access to music with headphones for individual students.
- An iPod can be a great way to access music during independent work. Underlying our state of arousal (or level of alertness) are internal rhythms, such as our heart rate and respiration. When we become unregulated from either an internal experience or something in our environment, our internal rhythms also become disorganized. For example, our heart rate quickens and our breathing becomes faster and shallower. Intuitively, we rock a baby to a steady rhythm when they become upset. Using music can help a disorganized body become calm and more organized as the internal body rhythms slow down and match the music's rhythms.
  - Examples from Therapeutic Listening include *Mozart for Modulation* CDs and *Baroque for Modulation* CDs; available through Vital Links (www.vitallinks.org)
  - Listening programs such as ILS (Integrated Listening System), the Tomatis method, Therapeutic Listening, and Listening Centre can also be helpful.
  - An FM system may be helpful in the classroom for a student who has been seen by an audiologist and found to have challenges screening out background auditory input.
- Try working while seated on dynamic cushions, therapy balls, or dynamic stools. Research has found that sitting on a therapy ball can help promote in-seat behavior as well as writing legibility. Classroom Seating for Children with Attention Deficit Hyperactivity Disorder: Therapy Balls. Versus Chairs Schilling, D. L., Washington, K., Billingsley, F. F, & Deitz, J. (2003). Classroom seating for children with attention deficit hyperactivity disorder: Therapy balls versus chairs. *American Journal of Occupational Therapy*, 57, 534-541.

Environmental Ideas to Help with Executive Functions
- Keep a standing folder by the student's desk so that as homework is assigned during the day, he or she can simply drop the homework into the standing folder and empty it into a knapsack at the end of the day.
- Keep work areas free of clutter– e.g., have pencil cases in desks to organize writing utensils, color-coded folders to help organize work for different classes.

- Keep a visual schedule handy to increase predictability and help with planning.
- Keep visual reminders, such as raise your hand to answer, within view to remind the student to make the right choice.
- Acknowledge success by hanging reward certificates near the student's desk. This can build the child's feelings of competency and self-esteem.
- Present steps of a new activity visually to help with sequencing.

Environmental Ideas to Help with Praxis, Including Body Awareness

- Have the student help clean up after an activity, which helps signal the end of the activity and can help with motor planning to understand the beginning, middle, and end of a given task; this will help students understand completion of a task.
- Outline physical space to help with body awareness. For instance, at circle time, have students sit on mats or inside hoola hoops. If they need to move a lot, they can also sit on a dynamic, air-filled cushion that they can wiggle on.
- Try to focus on one task at a time—reduce the need to multi-task and excessive motor planning demands.
- Review task demands with videos the student can watch to prepare for the performance.

Sensory Ideas to Incorporate throughout the School Day

Below are ideas you can try in your classroom to enable your students to modulate sensation and stay in the "just right" state. More time spent in the "just right" state means more time spent learning.

1. Bus Ride

Vestibular

- The bus or car ride can provide some great vestibular input; this linear forward/backward movement tends to have a calming effect on the body. However, if a student finds this input overwhelming, then try to incorporate "heavy work" to override any sensitivities (e.g., chewing gum if allowed or chewing on a chew tube, sucking on a sport water bottle, using a pull tube or stretchy band or silly putty).

Olfactory

- Favorite smells accessible in a small container can enable a student with a hypersensitive response to smells manage in an environment like a bus, which can have unpredictable smells.

Tactile

- Provide something to fidget with while seated (e.g., mini koosh ball, stress ball, mini slinky).
- Wearing a flannel vest or shirt can be calming to touch.
- Tactile ribbons can be tied to a knapsack.
- Provide a stuffed animal.

Proprioceptive

- A weighted item, such as a weighted lap-snake, can be worn on the student's lap or shoulders.
- If you live close enough to the school, you can walk. The walk itself can be quite regulating.
- Try hopping/galloping/stomping on the way to the bus.
- Wear a backpack that's weighted (plain old books seem to do the trick!). *Note:* This could place excess strain on the muscles and joints in students with low muscle tone.
- Try wearing a neoprene vest or band (you can also try a "waist trimmer," available in the sports section in department stores) around the lower ribs; not only does this provide great deep touch input (tactile system), but it also provides proprioceptive input when you breathe or move.

Visual

- Wear sunglasses.
- Wear colored glasses.
- Wear a baseball hat with a wide brim to reduce glare.

Auditory

- Listen to calming/relaxing music or white noise from an iPod to help drown out background noise.
- Use noise-cancelling headsets.
- Headsets designed for construction workers can also be tried.

Gustatory & Interoception

- Suck on candy or chew gum, if permitted
- If the student is slow to get going in the morning and does not have enough time to eat breakfast, if possible pack breakfast to go in a bag for the bus ride (if permitted) or for when entering school; try using juice boxes, sports water bottles with straws, or yogurt tubes because the sucking action can be quite organizing.
- Enable students to read the signs that their nervous system may be overwhelmed and encourage the use of sensory and communication strategies to return to the "just right" state of regulation.
- Things to watch out for include too much vestibular and auditory sensation, hunger, thirst, need to use the washroom, strong emotions about going to school, and difficulty regulating temperature.

Sensory-Based Motor Disorder: Posture
- Provide support when getting on/off the bus.
- Encourage the student to sit in a seat close to the door.
- Suggest waiting until other students have exited and cleared the hallway to the bus before getting up to leave.

Dyspraxia
- Have students review a social or video story prior to getting on the bus for the first time.
- Practice getting on/off a bus during the summer before school starts.
- Review activities that you can perform when riding on the bus (reading, singing not loudly, looking out the window, talking with a friend)

Executive Functions Supported by Efficient Sensory Processing
- Inhibition
- Emotional control
- Self-monitoring

2. Schoolyard Time/Recess

Vestibular

Movement activities can help promote attention and regulation. Therefore, movement before class can be quite helpful.

Some ideas:
- Jump rope
- Hopscotch
- Tag
- Basketball
- Simon Says
- Stop-and-go activities (e.g., What time is it, Mr. Wolf?)
- Kite flying
- Playground equipment if available—swings especially can be quite organizing
- Climbers, jungle gyms, slides, teeter-totters

Olfactory
- Access to preferred smells in a smell container can help a student deal with unpredictable smells of recess.

Tactile

- Sand or water play stations
- Tactile adventure bag—filled with lots of great items like squeeze ball, beanbag, Kooshball, slinky, etc.
- String games
- Building games
- Beading
- Gardening

Proprioceptive

- Animal walks (e.g., crabwalks, bear walks, frog jumps)
- Running
- Tag
- Kicking a soccer ball
- Yoga
- Baseball
- Walking/hiking
- Blowing bubbles
- Obstacle courses
- Playing catch
- Climbing

Visual

- Looking at a favorite book
- Kites
- Streamers
- Flashlight tag—if indoor recess, you can turn off the lights and track each other's lights on the ceiling
- Balloon volleyball (moves slowly)
- Making up dances with scarves
- Popping bubbles
- Blowing musical instruments (blowing helps organize vision)
- Chalk drawings or drawing hopscotch
- Playing board games

Auditory

- Listening to favorite music on headphones
- Dancing/moving to music
- Drumming or stomping to the rhythm of a song

- Dance Freeze—play music and everyone needs to freeze when someone pauses the music
- Musical Chairs (can play non-competitive versions too)
- Copying each other's tunes using whistles and musical instruments
- Earmuffs to help block out excess noise
- Warning students before the bell rings to help them prepare their nervous system for the sound

Gustatory

- Gum can provide great organizing "heavy work" for the mouth.
- Crunchy snacks can be a source of proprioceptive input and can have a calming and organizing effect on the body. Examples include carrot sticks, celery, pretzels, veggie chips, and rice cakes.
- Chewy snacks can be another source of organizing proprioceptive input. Examples include raisins, dried fruits, beef jerky, and bagels.

Interoception

- Enable students to read the signs that their nervous system may be overwhelmed and encourage the use of sensory and communication strategies to return to the "just right" state of regulation.
- Things to watch out for include too much auditory and tactile sensation, need to use the washroom, hunger, thirst, and strong emotions.
- Sensory-Based Motor Disorder: Posture -Come up with ideas for less complex physical games.
- Individual sports are easier to coordinate than team sports.
- Engage in pretend play.
- Practice games at home and transfer them to school.
- Bend down and reach up to collect items from outside, like leaves, and attach them to rings of tape to make a bracelet.
- Obstacle courses.

Dyspraxia

- Cause-and-effect toys are great for children who have challenges with motor planning.
- If the student seems aimless, try incorporating structure in activities, such as:
  - Obstacle course
  - Easy rope-skipping games
  - Easy games like Mother May I
  - 4 square—use tape on the ground or chalk
  - Hopscotch
  - Tether ball or tether balloon also keeps the ball within reach.
- Break down movement games into smaller components to ensure success.
- Games like zoom ball are great since the ball cannot fall off the ropes.

- Play catch with Velcro mitts.
- Blow bubbles.

Executive Functions Supported by Efficient Sensory Processing
- Inhibition
- Shifting
- Emotional control
- Initiation
- Working memory
- Planning/organization
- Organization of materials
- Self-monitoring

A note about recess: Recess time outside must be non-negotiable and should not be denied a child as punishment for misbehaving in class. Recess enables movement opportunities for children to move their bodies and regulate their nervous system. Some may need help in learning structured recess activities.
- To be successful at recess, it is important to explore the students':
- Motivators
- Sensory and motor strengths
- Sensory and motor challenges
- A "recess treasure chest" filled with toys the student already knows how to play with can make recess a success. Put the student in charge of who gets to play with him or her. Keep in mind that you may want to change the objects in the treasure chest to keep play interesting and playmates interested.
- Pair a student who may be finding recess challenging with a recess buddy. This can be an older student who is looking to gain experience working with children.
- Create friendship circles where children play with different friends each day of the week

If a child continues to face challenges at recess due to the unstructured time, extra sensory input, or social skills, try incorporating more vocation skills, such as:
- Photocopying
- Delivering milk/juice
- Gathering the recycling from the classes
- Cleaning the board or the windows
- Horticulture—digging, planting, raking leaves, shoveling snow (all great sources of sensory input and "heavy work!")
- Crafting
- Caring for a classroom pet

These vocational skills can be performed with a peer to make them social.

Additional resources:

Ramstetter, C. L., Murray, R., & Garner, A. S. (2010). The crucial role of recess in schools. *Journal of School Health*, 80 (11), pp. 517-526.

Barros, R. M., Silver, E. J., & Stein, R. E. K. (2009). School recess and group classroom behaviour. *Pediatrics* (123) 2, pp. 431-436.

3. Entering the School—Cubby/Locker Time

Vestibular

- Enter the school a few minutes before other students to transition to school without the balance demands of many students in a small space.
- Move outside the school to organize the nervous system prior to entering the school.

Olfactory

- Provide access to preferred smells in a smell container to help a student deal with the unpredictable smells of the cubby area or hallways.
- Put lotion on the hands/powder on the feet that has a favorite smell.

Tactile

- Position the cubby/locker at the end of the cubbies to minimize touch by other students.
- Come into the cubby/locker area a few minutes before the other students.
- Once in the classroom, having the student sit in a large beanbag chair in the corner of the classroom can provide some calming deep-touch input (available at Walmart or Ikea).
- You can make your own mini bean bags with fabric and aquarium gravel (so that they can be washed).
- Have tactile fidgets or a stuffed toy to touch during the beginning of the school day.

Proprioceptive

- Wear a weighted knapsack to help calm the body.
- Wear a compression vest/weighted vest.
- Wear ¼-pound weights on the wrists/ankles.
- Put a lap snake across the knees or over the shoulders.
- Push/pull/lift and carry mats for use in the circle.
- Do animal walks, early morning jumping jacks, or yoga stretches.

Visual
- Provide visuals—schedules, labels, sequence pictures.

Auditory
- For younger children, sing a song to cue the upcoming activities.
- Singing helps get everyone "on the same page."
- Headphones can be worn to minimize the escalating sound of children entering the classroom.
- Music can be played in the background.
- The child can be directed to the quiet corner at the beginning of the day.

Gustatory
- Crunchy chewy breakfast foods can help prepare the child for the school day.

Interoception
- Support students to read the signs that their nervous system may be overwhelmed and encourage the use of sensory and communication strategies to return to the "just right" state of regulation.
- Things to watch out for include too much auditory, visual, and tactile sensation, emotions about school, missing family members, anxiety, temperature regulation, need to use the washroom, hunger, or thirst.

Sensory-Based Motor Disorder: Posture
- Ensure that the environment is clear of obstacles and pathways in the classroom are open.
- Give the student a book bag to use to bring items to circle.
- Offer supportive seating at circle time (howda hug seats) or maybe even a small chair if necessary.
- Provide the child with enough space to sit down without falling on neighbors.

Dyspraxia
- Follow a visual schedule of steps to complete a task.
- Use counting, rhythm, or singing to help with motor planning.
- Offer a consistent schedule for each day to provide a sense of predictability.

Executive Functions Supported by Efficient Sensory Processing
- Inhibition
- Shifting
- Emotional control
- Initiation
- Planning/organization

- Organization of materials
- Self-monitoring

Other Information
- A compression vest adds deep pressure and provides input during breathing and moving. It may be preferred to a weighted vest as it does not increase the balance demand. Weighted vests may be preferred and the general rule for their wear is 20 minutes on and 20 minutes off to prevent the nervous system from growing accustomed to the sensation (habituation).
- A howda hug chair is like a concert seat for the lawn. It offers support to the back and rocking movement. It is available at www.howda.com.

4. *Settling into Classroom (Organization, Take Homework Out)*

Vestibular
- Walking to the desk
- Daily physical activity time which includes movement
- Yoga
- Seating that offers movement (mambo seat, hokki seat, air-filled cushion)

Olfactory
- Access to preferred smells in a smell container to help a student deal with unpredictable smells of the classroom
- Using smelly pencils, pens, markers

Tactile
- Access to fidget items, like a stress ball, putty, etc.
- Covering desktop, books, and pencils with textured fabric
- Offering soft cushions to sit on

Proprioceptive
- Activities that can be incorporated into daily physical activity times:
- Body stretches
- Animal walks
- Chair push-ups—hands at side of waist and push body up and down
- Chair pull-ups—hands below seat and lift up
- Chair push-out—legs between chair legs and put legs outward

- Chair pull-ins—feet on outside of chair legs and pull in and relax
- Desk hugs—stretch the arms out to grasp the top of the desk and hug it toward the body

Visual
- Schedule or reminders on the board, computer, or desk
- Timers set (if needed)

Auditory
- Classroom FM system to help students hear the teacher above the classroom noise
- Headphones to block out extra noise in the classroom
- Headphones with favorite music playing softly

Gustatory
- Snacks of crunchy, chewy foods

Interoception
- Support students to read the signs that their nervous system may be overwhelmed and encourage the use of sensory and communication strategies to return to the "just right" state of regulation.
- Things to watch out for include anxiety about the upcoming school day, need to use the washroom, and response to tactile, auditory, visual and vestibular sensation.

Sensory-Based Motor Disorder: Posture
- Offering supportive seating (a chair with arms can be very supportive)
- Having space around the student so that he or she doesn't bump into others
- Placing the desk at the end of the group to minimize bumping elbows
- Offering a weighted water bottle with a sports top to avoid spills

Dyspraxia
- Visual schedule to follow and check off all steps
- Visual sequence cards or videos to introduce new movements
- Ability to watch other students doing an action prior to doing it themselves
- Ability to ask for more time

Executive Functions Supported by Efficient Sensory Processing
- Inhibition
- Shifting
- Emotional control

- Initiation
- Working memory
- Planning/organization
- Organization of materials
- Self-monitoring

Other information
- A mambo chair and a hokki chair are mushroom-shaped chairs with a convex bottom that enable movement. They can be found at www.fdmt.ca and www.amazon.com.
- Smelly pencils, markers, and erasers can be found at most stationery stores.

5. Work
a. Listening to Teacher
b. Carpet Time

Vestibular
- Vestibular (movement/balance) activities prime the core muscles for sitting (jumping jacks, animal walks, marching, skipping, and galloping to the carpet).
- Movement can be as simple as taking a break and nodding the head yes and no or bending each ear to touch the closest shoulder.
- Supportive seating like a howda hug chair can support balance
- Placing child directly opposite the teacher if he or she is sensitive to moving the head
- If the child needs more movement, involve him or her in helping to run the circle

Olfactory
- Accessing preferred smells in a smell container to help a student deal with unpredictable smells of the classroom
- Putting on lotion or powder with a favorite scent at the beginning of carpet time

Tactile
- Have access to quiet fidget items to aid with regulation, such as mini koosh balls, silly putty, mini slinky, art gum erasers (much more flexible and pliable than typical erasers)
- Fill a balloon with flour to create your own fidget item,
- Other fidget toy ideas include scrunchy hair elastics, clothespins, pipe cleaners, Wikki Stix, fidget pencils with a fidget near the eraser end of the pencil, polished stones, coil shoelaces, Tangles, stress balls, hand lotion, etc.

- Try access to weighted items for short periods of time (maybe 20 minutes on and at least 20 minutes off) so the body does not get used to or habituate to the sensation
- Weighted items include weighted vest or weights around wrists or ankles, weighted lizard for the lap
- Create own weighted item by filling stuffed animals or socks with rice, beans, or aquarium gravel

Proprioceptive
- You can incorporate "heavy work" right into your lesson plans with a bit of creativity. For a math lesson, for example, have the numbers 1 through 10 written on cards on the floor in an arc around the student. Have the student lie on his or her stomach on the floor and blow a cotton ball or small ball of tissue using a straw to the correct number for the answer. This incorporates great "heavy work" through the postural muscles.
- Incorporate questions in class into an obstacle course. Have a student complete the obstacle course and at the end find a question and write the answer on the board. This incorporates periods of movement and proprioception sensation with a focus. It also offers writing on a vertical surface, which can be great position for those learning how to write.
- Work on practicing letter or number formation using playdough, clay, or putty. You can either roll it into a snake to form the letter or number or you can write in the dough using your index finger or a popsicle stick.
- Practice number, letter, and shape formation using many sensory modalities like goop, sand, and rice painting with water. Interesting sensations harness attention and can improve learning and memory of letter/number formation.

Visual
- Natural light can be quite valuable in promoting self-regulation
- Some people work best when everything around them is organized and put away. Other people function best in a visually chaotic environment.
- Offer the soft light of lamps instead of fluorescent lights
- Offer a laptop screen instead of a desktop screen
- Offer an easel so that the glare of overhead light isn't reflected into the eyes of the student
- Some people focus and learn best with visual sensation, glitter wands, an aquarium, or lava lamp
- Some students are visual learners and require visual instructions and demonstrations
- Some students learn best while doodling (which also has tactile and kinesthetic components)
- Promote personal space and boundaries with strategies such as having each student sit in a hoola hoop or on their own cushion/mat
- Some people focus much better with less visual input by wearing a hooded sweatshirt or baseball cap while studying

- Students who have difficulty integrating their fields of vision may have difficulty with spatial awareness (knowing where items are in relation to them) and may be startled by sudden movements
- Do not require students to look directly at you if doing so is uncomfortable for them
- Check-in chart for regulation skills

Auditory
- An FM system to help bring the teacher's voice into the forefront of the noises in the classroom
- Headphones to block out noise
- Familiar songs to signal the beginning of an activity

Gustatory
- Favorite snacks to affect arousal and attention

Interoception
- Support students to read the signs that their nervous system may be overwhelmed and encourage the use of sensory and communication strategies to return to the "just right" state of regulation.
- Things to watch out for include too much visual, auditory, tactile, and vestibular sensation, anxiety, emotion, or need to use the washroom.

Sensory-based Motor Disorder: Posture
- Introducing a wedge on the student's seat can help with alignment and posture, activate the inner core muscles, as facilitate the processing of sensory input from the environment more effectively
- Try air-filled cushions to sit on to help promote posture Try, for example, the Disc'o'sit cushion, Move'n'sit cushion, yoga disc, or slightly filled beach ball.
- A howda hug seat can support a child in sitting in the circle

Dyspraxia
- Access to a cushion or chair to sit on during circle time if getting up/down is challenging
- Access to a visual schedule or visual timer to give the student predictability
- Demonstration of the task or assignment first before independent work
- Familiar songs and activities to begin each circle

Executive Functions Supported by Efficient Sensory Processing
- Inhibition
- Shift
- Emotional control
- Working memory

- Planning/organization
- Self-monitoring

Other information

- Wikki Stix are wax-covered strings that can be formed into many shapes. They are available at most toy stores.
- Goop is made of cornstarch and water and is a solid when compressed and a liquid when the compression is released.
- One study found that doodling helped a group of people recall 29% more information on a memory test than those who did not (Andrade, J., "What does doodling do?," Applied Cognitive Psychology, 2009).
- An assessment by a behavioral optometrist is essential to understand how a student processes vision.
- The dynamic nature of the cushions will help promote constant input to the small muscles along the spine to stay engaged and the movement the cushion provides also promotes attention.
- The Incredible 5-Point Scale offers a great check-in sheet for morning circle time. Students can review their state of regulation and make choices to get into the "just right" state of regulation.
- Students can be taught scripts that they can use to functionally ask for more time: "I'm working on this!" or "I need a few more minutes please."

6. Work:
a. Independent Desk Work

Vestibular

- Sitting on an air-filled cushion to help promote movement, which in turn, helps with increasing attention and regulation (e.g., Disc'o'Sit Jr., Move'n'Sit Jr., yoga disc)
- Placing an air-filled cushion or a rocker board under your feet while working at the desk
- Working at a standing desk
- Sitting on a stool requires more postural control and uses more movement
- Try a dynamic stool such as the hokki stool or mambo seat
- Try a rocking chair
- Build in movement into the activities—for example, if completing an assignment that needs different colored pencil crayons, set them up across the classroom so that each time a new color is needed, the student has to get up and move across the class to retrieve it

- Try sitting on a gym ball—ensure that it's the correct size so that the student is seated with his or her feet flat on the floor and 90 degrees at the ankles, knees, and hips
- Try sitting on a t-stool which looks like a stool with one leg in the center for high balance demands
- Try putting an inflated tire inner tube on the seat of a chair for a student to sit on for a bouncy seating option or against the back of the chair to lean back against
- You can also try having a student seated on a therapy ball placed on a tire inner tube to help keep the ball from rolling away
- Two students can work together on spelling, math problems, or any subject while bouncing on therapy balls together—you can bounce with each letter while spelling a word or answer math questions with the number of bounces (e.g., bounce four times for an answer of four)

Olfactory
- Access to scented erasers, pencils, markers, and crayons
- Try different scented lip balms
- Tactile—Access to fidget items—e.g., putty, stress ball, mini slinky, etc.
- Access to beanbag chairs for calming deep-touch input
- Writing using a vibrating pen at times can be quite calming and organizing through its deep-touch input and regular rhythm
- Try including matching games with buckets or plastic bins filled with dry beans or dry rice. Students can match vocabulary words on their list to their definitions hidden in the bin or math questions to their answers hidden within

Proprioceptive
- Stretchy bands tied around the front legs of a chair can be used for the student to push his or her feet or legs against for proprioceptive input
- Working in alternative positions: standing and writing on a paper taped at eye level on the wall or working on an easel -working on your stomach while propped up on forearms at the floor
- Incorporating "heavy work" breaks, such as desk push-ups, wall push-ups, finger tug-of-war, animal walks, etc.
- If a child holds a pencil too tightly and uses excessive pressure while writing and drawing, he or she may have challenges processing proprioceptive input. You can try hand warm-ups before writing (e.g., stretching putty, yoga stretches, doodling). You can also try a weighted pencil which enables the student to learn how much pressure to exert during the task of writing by providing extra proprioceptive input.

Visual
- Fluorescent lights can be challenging for individuals with visual sensitivities; try a lamp instead

- Try wearing a baseball hat or sunglasses
- For students who are very visually distracted—try having them sit behind a study carrel while they do their work
- Offer smaller spaces, like inside a classroom tent for students to read
- Try writing on graph paper for math class to help with spacing/organization on the page
- Use a different colored binder for each subject to help with organization
- Try using an easel to prevent glare from reflected light
- Tape a number/letter line as a visual reference to the student's desk to support correct letter and number formation
- Many people who have visual sensitivities cannot look you directly in the eye while speaking. This does not imply that they are not listening. Instead of asking them to look at you, check in at times to ensure they have heard all the material.
- When learning individual letters, have students write the letter in a square and begin their letter on a symbol in the top-left corner to help prevent reversals
- A green dot on the left side of the line can signal to a student to return to the left side of the page and a red dot on the right side of the page can signal that it is time to start a new line
- Using a bubble pipe to blow through can be a great way to work on deep belly breathing and can help work on visual convergence, which could be useful before independent reading

Auditory
- Position desk in a quiet corner in the room to minimize background noise
- You may want to consider a "Central Auditory Processing Assessment" if the student has challenges in areas such as difficulty in a noisy environment, trouble responding to his or her name being called in a noisy setting, lots of difficulty with spelling, etc.
- Some individuals work best in a quiet environment such as a library whereas others work optimally in a noisier environment such as a coffee shop
- Our need for auditory input can change throughout the day; students may need quieter music early in the day and faster music after lunch

Gustatory
- Offer chewelery (chewable jewelry) or chewable pencil toppers if the student seems to be seeking oral-motor input
- Gum can be a great way to offer proprioceptive input around the mouth and promote attention
- Drinking water through a sports water bottle; the proprioceptive input provided by sucking can have a very calming and organizing effect on the body

Interoception
- Support students to read the signs that their nervous system may be overwhelmed and encourage the use of sensory and communication strategies to return to the "just right" state of regulation.
- Things to watch out for include anxiety about performance, hunger, thirst, too much tactile, visual, or vestibular sensation, or need to use the washroom.

Sensory-Based Motor Disorder: Posture
- Use of air-filled cushions
- Working in alternative positions
- Working on a tabletop easel can help promote upright posture
- Have students move! Have them kick or bounce a ball to each other in the hall while answering math questions—e.g., if the question is 6 x 2 they can kick the ball 12 times.

Dyspraxia
- Having a visual list of steps needed to complete
- It is common for people with dyspraxia to have challenges with handwriting:
- Try exploring different types of paper
- Pencil grips may be useful—you may want to consult an occupational therapist for more suggestions
- Access to a computer if trouble keeping up with class demands with handwritten assignments
- If the student finds it really challenging to keep up, consider looking at the quality rather than quantity of his or her written work; you can also use alternative methods to answer questions that require less writing, such as multiple choice questions, true or false questions, highlighting or circling answers
- Try using graph paper for math to help organize numbers and keep the rows of ones, tens, and hundreds in the correct place
- If the student has challenges with sequencing, try incorporating multi-sensory strategies or movement. For example, if a student is having trouble sequencing the letters of his or her name, have the student jump on hopscotch tiles in the room with letters in the name

Other information
- A student who is under-responsive to sensory input may have trouble focusing and determining what to pay attention to and what to screen out in a busy environment.
- Calming environments can be quite helpful for students with over-responsivity, such as:
- Hide-outs and small spaces
- Keep in mind the need for time and to re-group
- Opportunities for relaxation and reflection
- Materials that may be useful: beanbag chair, lower lights, fidgets items, etc.

- A weighted pencil can be purchased online or you can make one by putting nuts (as in nuts and bolts) on the end of the pencil and securing them with duct tape.
- If your student shows many letter and number reversals past 2nd grade, this can be related to challenges with spatial awareness and you may want to try a letter/number strip on the student's desk to look at while working. A referral to a behavior optometrist to rule out visual challenges is also suggested.
- Information about central auditory processing disorder can be found at http://www.capdsupport.org/Diagnosis/what-is-capd.html
- You can make your own tabletop easel by taping 2- to 3-inch binders together.

Executive Functions Supported by Efficient Sensory Processing
- Inhibition
- Emotional control
- Initiation
- Working memory
- Planning/organization
- Organization of materials
- Self-monitoring

7. Computer Use

Vestibular
- Dynamic seating to help promote vestibular input (and therefore attention and body awareness) while working at the computer
- Try placing the feet on an air cushion or rocker board

Olfactory
- Access to preferred smells in a smell container can help a student deal with unpredictable smells of the classroom
- Try different scented lip balms

Tactile
- Try a texture on the computer mouse
- Cover the desktop with a textured fabric that the student can touch
- Cover the chair with a textured fabric

Proprioceptive
- Use a weighted item (e.g., weighted lap snake) around your lap or shoulders while working at the computer
- Try a compression vest or weighed vest
- You may want to try a theraband around the front legs of the chair to help with focus/attention

Visual
- Play around with contrasting colors as some people can read better in color contrasts other than black text on a white background—you can invert the colors, use different colors, or use only grayscale
- Change the size of text shown on the computer's display
- Use the magnifier function
- Some people who are visually sensitive are more successful when viewing the computer screen from an angle instead of directly from in front. Anti-glare screens are available to place over the screen to help cut down on visual glare.
- You can change the size of the cursor
- Use special gloves with letters written on the fingertips or different colored letter stickers that you can stick on your fingers to help with touch typing (also helps with motor planning)
- Encourage the students to take frequent breaks when they look far away and rest the muscles of their eyes

Auditory
- Word prediction software to help with spelling challenges (such as WordQ or Read, Write, and Gold)

Gustatory
- Chewing gum, eating crunchy or chewy food prior to working on the computer

Interoception
- Support students to read the signs that their nervous system may be overwhelmed and encourage the use of sensory and communication strategies to return to the "just right" state of regulation.
- Things to watch out for include too much visual, vestibular, auditory, tactile sensation, need to use the washroom, and anxiety about performance.

Sensory-Based Motor Disorder: Posture
- Ensure that the student is seated with feet flat on the floor and at 90 degrees at the ankles, knees, and hips to increase the feeling of stability
- Desk should be 2" below the hands with elbows flexed when typing
- Supportive seating in a chair with arms

Dyspraxia
- Use speech recognition for the computer to write down your ideas or read back what has already been written to check for spelling or grammar errors
- Try typing games and programs to facilitate keyboarding skills if printing is challenging
- Examples include Qwertynomics, BBC Dance Mat Typing, Keyboarding Without Tears, Sense –Lang, Fun to Type, and Typing Tutor
- People with severe motor challenges can sometimes program tablets to use actions to access programs (e.g., pinch or swipe with one finger)

Executive Functions Supported by Efficient Sensory Processing
- Inhibition
- Shift
- Initiation
- Working memory
- Planning/organization
- Self-monitoring

Other information
- Some children may have difficulty with visual processing. An assessment by a behavioral optometrist (www.covd.org) or an Irlen screener may be helpful (www.irlen.com).

8. Lunch and Snacks

Vestibular
- Option to eat while standing at the desk or on a dynamic air-filled cushion
- Movement opportunities prior to eating to help regulate the nervous system

Olfactory
- If the smells of others' lunches are too overpowering for the student, try offering a spot at the corner of the class or cafeteria or in another room. Encourage the student to invite a friend.

Tactile
- If the student is sensitive to touch, have him or her sit in a position at the table that minimizes the chances of bumping into neighbors

- If the student is upset and oversensitive because of having food on his or her hands or face, have a towel handy for cleaning up. If you are cleaning the student's hands or face, use consistent touch and prior warning.
- Discomfort with the textures of food is real and need to be respected.
- Have tolerated foods on hand in case the student has a lunch he or she cannot tolerate.
- Offer water to clean out the mouth in between mouthfuls.

Proprioceptive
- Some people find crunchy foods quite organizing and calming. Examples include carrot sticks, celery sticks, apples, pretzels, and bagel chips.
- Some people find chewy foods quite regulating. Examples include bagels, dried fruits, and pepperoni sticks.
- If the student has challenges using utensils, try weighted utensils because they help strengthen students' awareness of their arm and hand.
- A student who is under-responsive to proprioceptive input may overfill his or her mouth with food and not notice how full it is—you can help support with eating in front of a mirror and speaking about the best size bites along with bites that are "too big" or "too small."
- Encourage drinking out of a straw for extra proprioceptive input.

Visual
- Consider the amount of visual input around a particular student when he or she is eating. If the student is quite visually sensitive, have him or her sit where there are no visual distractions.

Auditory
- Calming music in the background may be helpful
- Access to headphones to block out noise if the student finds it too loud.

Gustatory
- Be mindful of lunches sent for students with sensory processing challenges—they may not be able to tolerate certain tastes or smells.

Interoception
- Support students to read the signs that their nervous system may be overwhelmed and encourage the use of sensory and communication strategies to return to the "just right" state of regulation.
- Things to watch out for include too much gustatory, olfactory, visual, tactile, auditory, and vestibular sensation, nausea, headache, need to use the washroom, and anxiety.

Sensory-Based Motor Disorder: Posture

- Optimal seating—a chair that allows the student to sit with feet flat on the floor and at 90 degrees at their ankles, hips, and knees—use a footstool (or stack of books) under the feet if needed for postural support
- Air-filled cushions or dynamic seating may be helpful in promoting posture.
- Build up the handles of utensils with pipe insulation.

Dyspraxia

- Easy-to open food containers
- Possibly Dycem under the plate or bowl if utensils are needed as Dycem helps stabilize the plate in case the student has difficulty using two hands together.
- Utensils with thicker handles are sometimes easier to use (surround handles with pipe insulation).

Executive Functions Supported by Efficient Sensory Processing

- Inhibition
- Shift
- Emotional control
- Planning/organization
- Organization of materials
- Self-monitoring

Other Information

- Pipe insulation can be bought at any hardware store and is quite inexpensive (25 cents/yd)

9. Transitions
a. Between Subjects within Class
b. Between Different Classrooms

Vestibular

- Try having students walk around the classroom three times together before settling down together.
- Take the long way to increase vestibular sensation.

Olfactory

- Have student smell a favorite smell (held in a small container) during the transition.

Tactile

- Use a tactile transition object to hold to help with transitions as it is difficult to focus on an object and be anxious at the same time.

Proprioceptive

- Stretches
- Isometric exercises
- Examples include:
- Palm presses
- Desk push-ups
- Try wearing a compression band, neoprene vest, or weighted vest
- Deep breathing exercises during waiting

Visual

- Visual schedules
- Visual timers
- Map to new destination

Auditory

- Timers
- Music or songs during transitions can be quite helpful—especially if they have a strong rhythm—as it aids in predictability
- Try adding upholstery foam around the PA system in the class to reduce the volume if needed

Gustatory

- Things to chew on can be quite calming and organizing, such as chew tubes, chewlery, straws, gum (if permitted),
- Crunchy foods can also be quite organizing and alerting, such as popcorn, celery, pretzels, nachos and salsa

Interoception

- Support students to read the signs that their nervous system may be overwhelmed and encourage the use of sensory and communication strategies to return to the "just right" state of regulation.
- Things to watch for include too much gustatory, olfactory, visual, tactile, auditory, and vestibular sensation, nausea, headache, need to use the washroom, uncertainty, and anxiety.

Sensory-Based Motor Disorder Posture

- Support for transitional movements
- Have student stand at the front of the line and hold the door then follow the group
- Be at the end of the line when going up stairs so the group isn't held up
- Have a knapsack to carry needed items to keep hands free
- Take breaks whenever necessary

Dyspraxia

- Students should help clean up after themselves. Not only does this help with the cleanup of the room or activity, but it also helps develop motor planning by teaching and signals the end of an activity. This can also help with transitions.

Executive Functions Supported by Efficient Sensory Processing

- Inhibition
- Shift
- Initiation
- Planning/organization
- Organization of materials
- Self-monitoring

Other Information

- Excellent programs are available that can be used to help students increase their tolerance of the texture of food. One program is called the SOS Feeding Program (www.spdfoundation.net) An occupational therapist can be very helpful in this area.

10. Group Work

Vestibular

- Access to work on air-filled cushions
- Options to stand while working at a desk or to work in different positions like lying on the stomach propped up on the forearms

Olfactory

- Scented pencils, markers, crayons, and erasers

Tactile

- Access to tactile fidgets

Proprioceptive
- Try incorporating "heavy work" or movement breaks prior to group work, such as walking a few laps around the room or helping re-arrange the tables and desks.
- Try offering strategies for students to use while working in a group, such as stretchy bands tied around the front legs of their chair or an air-filled cushion to sit on to help provide extra proprioceptive input.

Visual
- Visual instructions to stay on task
- The components of the project displayed visually (often called a marking rubric)

Auditory
- Try working in a quiet corner of the class or in the hall
- Try headphones with no music or calming music

Gustatory
- Crunchy or chewy snacks can help with attention
- Lemon/orange or cucumber water in a sports top bottle

Interoception
- Support students to read the signs that their nervous system may be overwhelmed and encourage the use of sensory and communication strategies to return to the "just right" state of regulation.
- Things to watch out for include too much olfactory, visual, tactile, auditory, and vestibular sensation, nausea, headache, need to use the washroom, and anxiety.

Sensory-Based Motor Disorder Posture
- Supportive seating (howda hug when working on the floor) and stable seat (with arms) when working at a table
- Movement breaks

Dyspraxia
- Visual sequence cards for a project
- Visual demonstrations prior to performance
- Time to process requests
- Choice of activity

Other Information
- For students with sensory over-responsivity, assign a buddy rather than a group.

- A student who has challenges processing proprioceptive input may have challenges knowing where his or her body is in space. These students can lack appropriate feedback from their muscles and joints. As a result, they may appear clumsy. They may touch everything they pass in the environment to give them a reference point for where they are in relation to the space around them. They may also unintentionally lie or work in a neighboring students' space.

Executive Functions Supported by Efficient Sensory Processing
- Inhibition
- Emotional control
- Initiation
- Working memory
- Planning/organization
- Organization of materials
- Self-monitoring

11. Gym Class

Vestibular
- This area is full of vestibular sensation.
- Students who are hyper-responsive may choose individual sports where they always stay on the ground (e.g., golf).

Olfactory
- Access to a preferred smell in a container, especially in the change room
- Students may have to change in another room if the smell is too strong
- Students may need a change of clothing if they cannot tolerate the smell of their gym clothes

Tactile
- Try wearing Lycra sportswear under jeans or sweatpants if inconsistent touch input leads to hyper-sensitive reactions.
- If a student is defensive to touch, try games that keep distance between players—e.g., badminton, track and field.
- Be mindful of the clothing needed for gym class—could the tags bother the student? What about elastic waistbands or ankle bands?

Proprioceptive
- Incorporate lots of "heavy work" activities in the class to help keep everyone regulated, especially prior to transitioning to the next class.
- Try small weights around the wrists or ankles to increase proprioceptive input—switch them every five minutes or so to avoid habituating (or getting used to) the input and therefore ignoring it.
- Scooter board activities
- Soccer
- Volleyball
- Rock climbing
- Swimming

Visual
- Try to reduce extra visual input when possible—e.g., mats on the wall in one color instead of multiple colors
- Try wearing a baseball cap

Auditory
- Try noise-cancelling headphones
- Try organizing music in the background to keep the class regulated
- Be aware of the noise volume as it tends to echo in large rooms where gym tends to take place

Gustatory
- Crunchy or chewy snacks prior to gym class may help with attention.

Interoception
- Support students to read the signs that their nervous system may be overwhelmed and encourage the use of sensory and communication strategies to return to the "just right" state of regulation.
- Things to watch out for include too much olfactory, visual, tactile, auditory, and vestibular sensation, nausea, headache, need to use the washroom, hunger, thirst, and anxiety.

Sensory-Based Motor Disorder Posture
- Notice what type of surface the activities are taking place on
- Kicking a ball can be a great way to work on weight-shifting and the ability to balance and stand on one foot while kicking with the other foot

Dyspraxia

- Provide visual instructions to help support verbal instructions (e.g., visuals on board or demonstrate a game or action first)
- Access to mirrors if possible to help provide extra visual feedback on actions/movements
- Use music/sounds/counting to support learning of new movements
- Break down sports into small steps to facilitate learning
- Attach language to movement and use games like Simons Says, musical chairs, and obstacle courses to promote body awareness
- Increase the challenge as needed for that "just right challenge"—for example—with Simon Says you can incorporate directional cues such as one jump to the left, walk backward, left hand on the head and right hand on the hip, etc.
- Adding weight to parts of the body can help strengthen the student's sense of body awareness—for example, wearing a compression vest or weighted vest during Simon Says or an obstacle course or trying weights on the ankles and wrists—make sure to switch the weights every few minutes so that the student does not habituate and stop paying attention to the input.
- Work on grading force with activities—e.g., throw a ball or beanbag to a closer target vs. a more distant target
- Learning new strokes in swimming can be a great way to work on motor planning and can also be fairly challenging if the student has motor planning difficulties

Other Information

- If a student is overwhelmed by all the sensation around him or her in the gym, try to move the student to a smaller room.
- Also, offer a lot of activities with resistance.
- Moving on uneven surfaces (like pavement or crawling on pillows) requires the student to use more feedback and feedforward mechanisms to maintain an upright posture and involves more unpredictable movements as he or she adjusts the body to changes in the underlying surface.

Executive Functions Supported by Efficient Sensory Processing

- Inhibition
- Emotional control
- Initiation
- Working memory
- Organization of materials
- Self-monitoring

12. Art Class

Vestibular

- Sitting on a moving cushion or seat
- Working at an easel while standing for more movement
- Supportive seating for those with balance challenges
- Keep work in line with eyes while the head is in neutral to decrease looking down and up

Olfactory

- Add a preferred scent to the paint
- Use smelly pencils/markers/crayons/erasers
- If sensitive to smell, have access to a container of a preferred smell

Tactile

- If a student is touch sensitive, be aware of this in planning projects—e.g., offer markers rather than paint, painting with a paintbrush rather than fingers, beading rather than clay, etc.
- Access to gloves during messy projects if the student is touch sensitive
- If the student seeks out touch, try moon-sand, sand art bottles

Proprioceptive

- Clay
- Play Dough
- Movement breaks carrying heavy objects
- Working with a lap snake on the lap or across the shoulders
- Working with weights on the wrists

Visual

- Wear a baseball hat or sunglasses if sensitive to overhead light glare
- Work on a slanted easel
- Work near the window for natural light
- Add sparkles to paint if there is a need for more visual sensation

Auditory

- Listen to music or white noise through a headset
- Block sound with noise-canceling headsets
- Muffle sounds with ear muffs

Gustatory
- Crunchy or chewy foods prior to art class can help attention.

Interoception
- Support students to read the signs that their nervous system may be overwhelmed and encourage the use of sensory and communication strategies to return to the "just right" state of regulation.
- Things to watch out for include too much olfactory, visual, tactile, auditory, and vestibular sensation, headache, need to use the washroom, hunger, thirst, and anxiety.

Sensory-Based Motor Disorder Posture
- Try air-filled cushions to sit on to help promote posture, –such as Disc'o'sit cushion, Move'n'sit cushion, yoga disc, or slightly filled beach ball.

Dyspraxia
- Try using a weighted pencil /paintbrush, sculpting knife

Other Information
- Have a video or demonstration outlining the steps of the task
- Encourage the student to request more time if necessary
- Try incorporating activities that use breath into art class. For instance, give each student three straws and have the students cut them in half and wrap an elastic band around them to keep them together. Fill a dish with bubble solution or dish detergent with a bit of food coloring and have them dip the straws in the dish and blow bubbles onto a piece of paper to make bubble designs.
- The dynamic nature of the cushions will help promote constant input to the small muscles along the spine to stay engaged and the movement the cushion provides also promotes attention.

Executive Functions Supported by Efficient Sensory Processing
- Inhibition
- Emotional control
- Initiation
- Working memory
- Planning/organization
- Organization of materials
- Self-monitoring

13. Music Class

Vestibular
- Move to the music!
- Offer supportive seating when movement is difficult to process
- Put the sheet music in the line of sight to minimize the demand of moving the head up and down

Olfactory
- Have a preferred scent available to mask any unexpected scents in music (many of the wind instruments can be smelly so suggest a string instrument to someone with sensitivity to smells)

Tactile
- There are many tactile experiences using the instruments
- If touch is challenging to process, use tools like drum sticks

Proprioceptive
- Practice grading force by practicing loud vs. soft drumming
- Reed instruments (such as clarinet, recorder, and flute) are great for working on controlling breath, which is important for regulation and can be useful for strengthening mouth musculature (e.g., may even help reduce difficulties with drooling)
- Instruments such as the tuba also incorporate a lot of "heavy work" on regulating breath, and when in a marching band, also incorporates movement

Visual
- Wear a baseball hat or sunglasses if the student is sensitive to visual input
- Move a conductor stick with ribbons if the student requires more visual stimulation

Auditory
- Access to headphones or earplugs if sound sensitive

Gustatory
- Crunchy or chewy foods prior to art class can help attention

Interoception
- Sports bottle filled with flavored water

- Support students to read the signs that their nervous system may be overwhelmed and encourage the use of sensory and communication strategies to return to the "just right" state of regulation.
- Things to watch out for include too much olfactory, visual, tactile, auditory, and vestibular sensation, headache, need to use the washroom, hunger, thirst, and anxiety.

Sensory-Based Motor Disorder Posture
- Supportive seating for children with balance challenges
- Movement breaks for students with endurance challenges

Dyspraxia
- Visual sequence pictures/videos to demonstrate how to stand for singing or the finger placement for an instrument

Executive Functions Supported by Efficient Sensory Processing
- Inhibition
- Emotional control
- Working memory
- Planning/organization
- Self-monitoring

14. Library

Vestibular
- Seated on a dynamic seat or cushion
- Possibility of standing while reading

Olfactory
- Carry a small container of a preferred scent in case there is an unexpected smell
- Offer the student the opportunity to move out of the room and away from the smell

Tactile
- Cover the books in a tactile jacket to engage the tactile system while the student is reading
- If the student cannot manage touch from other students, encourage the student to work at his or her own desk to minimize unexpected touch

Proprioceptive
- Helping to carry and hand out books
- Re-stocking library shelves

Visual
- Sitting in a spot in the library that has few visual distractions
- A ruler or rectangle cut out of thick paper or cardboard to help keep track of the student's spot as he or she reads and to help block out the extra visuals on the page
- Be mindful of the light glare
- Wear a baseball hat or glasses to minimize visual demands

Auditory
- Wear headphones with music or white noise
- Ear muffs or noise-canceling headsets to block out extra sound

Gustatory
- Chewing gum (if allowed) or sipping water through a sport water bottle

Interoception
- Support students to read the signs that their nervous system may be overwhelmed and encourage the use of sensory and communication strategies to return to the "just right" state of regulation.
- Things to watch out for include too much olfactory, visual, tactile, auditory, and vestibular sensation, headache, need to use the washroom, hunger, thirst, and anxiety.

Sensory-Based Motor Disorder Posture
- Enable changes in position
- Enable movement breaks to deal with fatigue
- Offer supportive seating

Dyspraxia
- The planning involved in reading is minimal but putting books away and lining up to go back to class involves planning. Have the student observe other students prior to the demand that students put their books away or line up.

Executive Functions Supported by Efficient Sensory Processing
- Inhibition
- Emotional control

- Working memory
- Organization of materials
- Self-monitoring

15. Special Events: Assemblies and Field Trips

General Tips

- The use of social stories can be helpful in the processing of sensation as it enables the child to predict what is going to happen and what he or she needs to pay attention to and what can be ignored.
- Vestibular-Movement warm-up prior to leaving for field trip to help prepare for the field trip or prior to sitting at assemblies
- Bring an air-filled cushion to an assembly to help with sitting tolerance
- Be mindful of sensory overload from other sensory channels
- Offer stable seating for assemblies; during transitions, have someone walk beside the student for extra stability

Olfactory

- Wear a necklace with a bottle of a favorite scent (e.g., coffee, mint, cinnamon, lavender)
- Citrus peel or other scent in a ziplock bag that can be held in a pocket
- If parent wears perfume or cologne, have cotton ball with parent's preferred scent
- Lip gloss, gum, hand lotion, and essential oils can help override smells that are perceived negatively. The student can choose his or her favorite scents.

Tactile

- Bring a small fidget items to touch

Proprioceptive

- Bring weighted items such as a weighted lap snake
- Wear a compression vest or weighted vest

Visual

- Help the student prepare for the change in routine with visual schedules
- Baseball hat with a wide brim to block out extra visuals
- Sunglasses
- Fidget item that is lit and moves
- Water/oil toys or glitter wands

Auditory

- Bring music player (such as iPod) with music that calms the student
- Try over-the-ear headsets instead of earbuds
- Noise-canceling headsets can be helpful
- You can also try earmuffs

Gustatory

- Have snacks that the student prefers in case he or she can't tolerate the tastes being offered
- The smells of food can travel so be cognizant and if available have an alternate place to eat or sit near open door or window
- Have water available to rinse out the mouth

Interoception

- Support students to read the signs that their nervous system may be overwhelmed and encourage the use of sensory and communication strategies to return to the "just right" state of regulation.
- Things to watch out for include too much olfactory, visual, tactile, auditory, and vestibular sensation, fatigue, need to use the washroom, hunger, thirst, and anxiety.

Sensory-Based Motor Disorder Posture

- Give support to student when he or she is changing positions
- Bring supportive seating if students are expected to sit for long periods of time
- Provide movement breaks to help manage fatigue

Dyspraxia

- Provide a social story/video story that can be watched prior to the assembly or field trip that outlines expectations
- Offer the opportunity to watch other students before the expectation to perform
- Break larger movements into smaller components

Executive Functions Supported by Efficient Sensory Processing

- Inhibition
- Shift
- Emotional control
- Planning/organization
- Self-monitoring

16. Homework

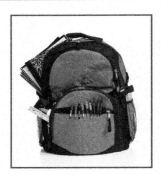

Vestibular
- Seated on a dynamic cushion or chair
- Work while standing
- Work in a rocking chair if available
- Work on a rocker-board

Olfactory
- Use scented pencil or scented erasers when completing homework

Tactile
- Access to fidgets while working (e.g., putty, stress ball, mini slinky, etc.)

Proprioceptive
- Theraband tied around front legs of chairs to push feet or front of legs against
- Movement breaks between work—e.g., wall push-ups, crabwalk, help carry laundry, help carry groceries to the kitchen, raking leaves, shovel snow, jumping on the bed

Visual
- Use visuals to support attention: visual-timer, visual schedule

Auditory
- Have calming background music on while completing homework
- Use auditory cues with a strong rhythm when learning how to form letters and numbers correctly
- Use mnemonics to help remember materials
- Use counting and rhyming during learning

Gustatory
- Access to crunchy snacks, chewy foods, alerting foods, sport water bottle, gum, etc.

Interoception
- Support students to read the signs that their nervous system may be overwhelmed and encourage the use of sensory and communication strategies to return to the "just right" state of regulation.
- Things to watch out for include too much olfactory, visual, tactile, auditory, and vestibular sensation, fatigue, need to use the washroom, hunger, thirst, and anxiety.

Sensory-Based Motor Disorder Posture
- Work in alternative positions—e.g., on easel, with chalk on sidewalk, on stomach propped up on fore-arms

Dyspraxia
- Break tasks into small components
- -Have visual steps of each task to follow

Executive Functions Supported by Efficient Sensory Processing
- Inhibition
- Shift
- Initiation
- Working memory
- Planning/organization
- Organization of materials
- Self-monitoring

17. Toileting

Vestibular
- Feet touching the floor
- Use of a toilet seat to make the opening smaller
- Stabilizing bars on the wall beside the toilet

Tactile
- Use wet wipes instead of toilet paper; they are more efficient
- Have good paper towels to wipe all the water off after washing hands

Olfactory
- Flush the toilet right away to minimize smells
- Have a preferred scent in a container to smell while in the washroom
- The handwashing station may need to be outside the washroom if the smell is too strong

Proprioceptive
- Deep pressure activities while sitting on the toilet, like a massage, may be helpful to relax the student
- Wear a compression vest during toileting for deep pressure input
- Wear ankle weights

Visual

- Have items, like books, to look at in the washroom
- If visual input is overwhelming, remove posters and pictures
- Have an aquarium light to increase relaxation

Auditory

- Washrooms can echo; try headphones
- Try noise-canceling headphones
- Singing may help your student relax

Gustatory

- Eating may stimulate the need to use the washroom

Interoception

- Support students to read the signs that their nervous system may be overwhelmed and encourage the use of sensory and communication strategies to return to the "just right" state of regulation.
- Things to watch out for include too much olfactory, visual, tactile, auditory, and vestibular sensation, fatigue, inability to use the washroom, hunger, thirst, and anxiety.

Sensory-Based Movement Disorder

- Ensure the student feels supported on the toilet
- Use a toilet seat to make the opening smaller
- Make sure the feet are on the floor

Dyspraxia

- Have a visual schedule of steps of the activity
- Watch a video outlining the steps
- Give adequate time

Other Information

- YouTube is a great source for videos of everyday activities
- You can also film your own
- Be aware that sometimes even the sound of the toilet flushing can be very dysregulating for a person with auditory processing challenges. Try using a washroom with only one toilet when possible to limit the amount of noise.
- If the student cannot tolerate the electric hand dryer, put an out-of-order sign on it when the student is using the toilet and take the sign off when you leave.

http://spdfoundation.net/MillerArticles/Sept.-Oct.%202012%20-%20SBMD,%20Dyspraxia.pdf
http://spdfoundation.net/MillerArticles/Jul.-Aug.%202012%20-%20SBMD,%20PD.pdf
http://spdlife.org/aboutspd/senses/interoception.html

Approach

The approach we use with people can also have a significant impact on their behavior. Here are some ideas to try:

General Regulation Approach Ideas:
- We must always be mindful of how we speak about students in front of them. We need to be aware that students pick up everything around them regardless of their level of understanding or verbal ability.
- Focus on the strengths of the student. We are all trained to focus on the students' challenges—change the focus to the positive!
- Behaviors are clues and they give us information about what the student needs.
- Notice that self-soothing behaviors serve a purpose. We cannot stop them without figuring out what purpose they serve and replacing with something else appropriate.
- Remember that neurons that fire together, wire together. Therefore, practicing activities with the just-right challenge when a student feels calm and regulated can help build strength and speed in the wiring of those messages/networks.
- When we find what works for a given student, it is important to write that information down and share with others involved in the student's life. Not only do we want to ensure that other teachers and family members can also use helpful strategies, but we also want to ensure that recommendations are passed on from a teacher from one year to the next so that they do not need to start from square one
- Try to schedule calming/organizing activities before and between more challenging tasks to help the student maintain a more organized nervous system.
- Incorporate a regulation program into your class. Several regulation programs are available, including:
  - The Alert Program
  - The Incredible 5-Point Scale
  - The Zones of Regulation
    These programs use cognitive skills to help identify different states of the body and emotions and choose strategies to help students remain in a calm, alert, and learning state. They are great when used with an entire class.
- Teach and explain sensory strategies to peers to foster success and understanding.

Transition Ideas:

- Help students maintain their focus away from anxiety by offering them a transitional object since the nervous system cannot focus on a motivating object and be anxious at the same time. "Transitional objects" can be quite useful to help with transitions. These are objects that the person can hold as he or she transitions to the next activity and are often related to that next activity e,g., carrying a book as you walk to the library, a piece of chalk as you walk to the chalkboard, or a snack as you leave for recess.

Ideas for a vestibular approach:

- Your brain learns best by doing! The more a student feels a sensation or completes an action, the more it hardwires in the brain for lasting memory.
- We learn using mirror neurons, which allows our brain to match the movements we observe to the movements we ourselves can perform (Rizzolatti & Sinigaglia, 2006). Therefore, students sometimes need time to stop and observe before trying something themselves. This can also be helpful to keep in mind when trying to teach appropriate social skills—model them. Video can also be used to demonstrate a new movement.
- Keep in mind that you want the student's body in optimal alignment to benefit from the sensory input he or she is receiving. Otherwise, the full impact of that sensation may not fully translate to the person's brain for processing. You may want to consult an occupational therapist, physiotherapist, or osteopath for more ideas.
- Be mindful that the vestibular system provides input to the eyes that helps them stay stable to see. Therefore, priming the body with movement activities prior to desk work can be helpful before activities such as reading and writing.

Ideas for a visual approach:

- Keep in mind that we have two streams for processing vision: We use our central vision for detail, color, and contrast and we use our peripheral vision for contrast, movement, and light information. We typically use these two systems simultaneously. Some people, however, tend to rely on their peripheral vision more than their central vision, especially if they are hyper-sensitive to visual sensation. Many individuals with autism are much better at processing information visually using their peripheral vision. Occupational therapists and teachers have observed that some students are better able to take things in visually when they or the object is in motion and they are using their peripheral visual system. Some people may find it difficult to use direct eye contact while communicating with you, perhaps because they are very sensitive when using the more sensitive central field of vision.
- Many individuals find it easier to rely on visual input from one eye alone if both their eyes are not working together effectively.

- Some individuals cannot process both visual input (looking at someone) and auditory input (listening to someone) at the same time. As a result, they may look away while someone speaks to them. Therefore, it may be useful to have a signal for students to show they are attending instead of asking them to look directly at you.

- Use visuals, such as visual timers, to alert the student of the beginning and end of an activity (e.g., Time Timer).

- Be aware of the clothing you wear around certain students; sometimes wearing neutral clothing with a given person can be helpful especially if the person has visual sensitivities. For instance, the person may have challenges being around a loud shirt with contrasting polka dots or stripes. Other times our clothing can help capture the attention of someone with visual challenges and "ground" the person in the environment. Also, be aware of how students respond to the different colors around them.

- Consider using social stories, which can be helpful in visually explaining how to act in different social situations—See Carol Gray's website for more information (www.carolgraysocialstories.com, www. thegraycenter.org)

Ideas for an auditory approach:

- Give the person time to process the instructions and react appropriately; often it's helpful to use a script such as "Whenever you're ready you can..."

- If your working memory is full of sensation waiting to be processed, you will need time to change gears and finish processing and engage a motor plan for a new activity. This can be supported visually, too.

- Notice your tone of voice. A student who is over-responsive will be most successful when spoken to in a quieter voice. However, a student who is under-responsive may be most engaged with a louder and more animated voice.

- A person may respond best to a sing-song voice that incorporates rhythm. Rhythm can help to compartmentalize sound into predictable chunks for processing.

Ideas for a proprioceptive approach:

- When you don't know what to try, try something that provides proprioceptive input.

- Movement against resistance can provide the nervous system with information regarding the body's position in space and sensation for regulation.

- Using a proprioception activity prior to an activity that requires more focus can be very helpful for some students

- Using a proprioception activity prior to a transition can help prepare the nervous system for the new sensation of the transition.

Ideas for a gustatory approach:

- Gustatory strategies can be used when a student is under-aroused; for example, dried mango strips which are tart and sweet can increase the level of arousal.
- Crunchy foods can have an alerting effect on our arousal.
- Taking sips of water during an activity can maintain levels of arousal.

Ideas for an olfactory approach:

- Keep in mind that our sense of smell is processed differently than any other sensory system as it's processed close to the limbic system, which is involved in memory and emotion. Our sense of smell can serve to help protect us. Also, when we are stressed, we can seek out or avoid smells. When our other senses are not working well, we tend to rely even more on our sense of smell. We may block smell if the sensory input is too much. Keep in mind the effect of cleaning products, perfumes, and shampoos/soaps, as well as the impact of possible allergies, chronic sinus challenges, etc.

General Regulation Ideas

- Be mindful that the structures organized in the midline of the body, such as the forehead, nose, mouth, and genitals, can have a strong modulating effect on the nervous system. A student who is sucking and chewing on the collar of his or her shirt or the end of a pencil may be trying to organize with this midline activity.
- We can also keep this idea of midline structures as regulating by helping students who are feeling dysregulated get into positions with more flexion (e.g., seated on a beanbag with knees bent into the chest). This can also help the eyes with convergence to focus on a point in front of them.
- When a student is overwhelmed and in coping mode, for example, if he or she is over-responding to the ticking of the new clock in the room, the flicker from the fluorescent light that is close to burning out, or the expectation that a substitute teacher will come in that afternoon, the student may ignore any input that is not related to the threat. That is one reason the student may look like he or she is unable to attend.
- When trying to figure out what types of activities may work to help a student regulate his or her body, keep in mind the inputs:

- Rhythm ➔ rhythmic activity tends to be calming (e.g., sitting in a rocking chair or bouncing on a therapy ball). Arrhythmic activities tend to be alerting (e.g., games like Red Light—Green Light).
- Intensity ➔ e.g., how intense is the sensation? Does this student love to swing as high as possible or keep his or her feet touching the ground?
- Frequency ➔ how often does the student engage in the activity throughout the day to support regulation? Some days that are more unpredictable may need a higher frequency of calming sensory activities.
- Duration ➔ how long does the student engage in a sensory activity? Does the student need it before transitions or all day?

  All these components will influence how effective the sensory activity is for your student.
- Incorporating "heavy work" activities, which tend to have a calming/organizing effect on the body, throughout a student's day can also be very regulating. Don't forget about chores and duties in the classroom. These activities are a source of heavy work and the pride in helping is a wonderful side effect!
  - Dragging or carrying recycling out of the class
  - Helping to collect and/or move bags of leaves
  - Pulling out big weeds from the garden
  - Shoveling snow
  - Wiping off the board
  - Washing the board
  - Stacking chairs and moving desks for group work
  - Carrying stacks of books to another room
  - Moving a television on a cart from one room to another
  - Pulling the wagon of milk at lunch time
  - Holding open the door for students to pass
- Try to use predictability and follow visual schedules to help the student predict what will be expected of him or her.
- When possible, try to help the student anticipate challenging situations (e.g., a fire drill).
- Provide opportunities for the student to calm his or her body, such as a hideout in the corner of the classroom (like a tent, beanbag chair, or space with soft cushions and softer lighting) or access to bins with sensory activities the student finds calming (tactile bin filled with dry beans and treasures hidden inside? Vibrating toys? Exercise bands?)
- Use social stories to help explain situations—look on Carol Gray's website for more information (www.carolgraysocialstories.com, www.thegraycenter.org
- Provide choices or options when possible
- Help provide feedback on how the student's body is running—e.g., "Your body looks like it's having trouble focusing right now and seems quite tired, maybe let's try..." Focusing on the student's body

or nervous system can be easier for the student. If we say YOU look like you need a break, it can be perceived as more personal or even as criticism.

- Use of visual timers, such as Time Timers, for example, give visual information on how much time for a given activity is left (www.fdmt.ca, www.toystoolsandtreasures.com).

Strategies for Co-Regulation

Co-regulation is the ability to become regulated by another person who is well regulated. Developmentally, we learn how to self-regulate, or the ability to attain, maintain, or change our level of alertness as appropriate to the situation, by being co-regulated by another person first. In fact, from birth to three months parents help co-regulate their baby by modulating their sleep-wake cycles, their hunger, as well as non-verbal communication and emotions.

- Be aware of how your voice can affect a particular student: tone, volume, speed, etc.
- Notice the position of your body in relation to the student.
- Song, rhythm, counting—the rhythms used in these can help regulate the rhythms in a student. Try matching the student's speed at first and then slowing down to a slower pace. This works because we all have internal rhythms in our body, such as our respiration and heart rates.
- Teach the student cognitive/language strategies:
  - "I need a minute" or "I need a break."
  - Have a hand gesture to signal unobtrusively to the student that his or her body is becoming disorganized and to choose a strategy to help regulate.
- Copy the words of the individual when reflecting back what is said to you.

Important points about our sense of smell:

- Our sense of smell is very powerful as the sensory input is not filtered before being processed in our brain; it goes directly to the middle brain and limbic system (associated with emotions and memory).
- Smell is invisible and we cannot see it coming.
- If someone has experienced trauma, he or she may react unpredictably to smells that remind of the traumatic event.

Calming Strategies

Deep Breathing

If you notice a student often seems to be on "high guard," anxious, or easily upset, you may want to try deep breathing, which can work wonders to calm a person's entire body, both physically and emotionally. Not only does it help slow down breathing rates which tend to quicken when we are stressed, but it also helps provide more oxygen to our body and free up our diaphragm to be used for deep breathing rather than recruited for other tasks like maintaining posture. Here are some ideas to incorporate deep breathing in the day. Try to practice when students are calm so that they have the skills ready to use when they are feeling anxious:

- Practice belly breathing together. Start with your hands on your belly to ensure that you are breathing through your belly instead of using shallow chest breathing. Breathe in through your nose, hold the breath for about three seconds, and let the breath out as slowly as possible through the mouth.
- Yoga
- Meditation
- Apps or online programs such as:
  - GoNoodle (https://www.gonoodle.com)
  - Headspace (https://www.headspace.com)
  - Breathe2relax (https://itunes.apple.com/ca/app/breathe2relax/id425720246?mt=8)
  - Ocarinia (http://www.smule.com/ocarina/original)
- Blowing bubbles
- Blowing a pinwheel
- Blowing a feather across the desk
- Use the Hoberman Sphere to teach breathing—see this link for more details: http://www.nationalautismresourcesblog.com/2013/10/27/how-to-teach-deep-breathing-to-children/

For more reading:

- Brown, R.P., & Gerbarg, P.L. Yoga breathing, meditation, and longevity. *Annals of the New York Academy of Sciences*, (1172), pp. 54-62.
- Brown, R. P., & Gerbarg, P. L. Sudarshan Kriya yogic breathing in the treatment of stress, anxiety, and depression: Part I—neurophysiologic model. *Journal of Alternative and Complementary Medicine*, 11(1), pp. 189-201.
- Brown, R.P., & Gerbarg, P.L. Sudarshan Kriya yogic breathing in the treatment of stress, anxiety, and depression: Part II—Clinical applications and guidelines. *Journal of Alternative and Complementary Medicine*, 11(4), pp. 711-717.

Mindfulness

Mindfulness, which has roots in Buddhist meditation, has spread widely to spiritual, religious, and secular settings. Jon Kabat-Zinn is a professor emeritus of medicine at the University of Massachusetts Medical School, where he was the founding executive director of its world-renowned Stress Reduction Clinic. According to Kabat-Zinn, mindfulness is a particular way of paying attention and involves our ability to pay attention in the present moment ("Full Catastrophe Living" by Jon Kabat-Zinn, pp. 11–12). Mindfulness involves concentrating on the immediate present experience instead of thinking and worrying about the future, judging what you are doing or have done in the past, or trying to exert control in your life (Leahy, Robert "The worry cure: Seven steps to stop worry from stopping you" (2005). Kabat-Zinn described mindfulness as an alternative to wasting energy reacting automatically and unconsciously to our environment and inner experiences and instead focusing that energy so that we can learn to calm our body and enter into deep relaxation in which we can see things in our life with greater perspective (pp. 11–12). This leads to better problem solving, rather than cycles of worry.

Anxiety and sensory processing challenges are often intertwined. Anxiety can magnify sensory processing challenges and sensory processing difficulties can lead to greater levels of anxiety. Mindfulness offers a great way to work on reducing anxiety for students to help maximize their ability to learn and play at school. Not only can teachers be certified in mindfulness from different programs, but some great apps are also available that can be used as moments to pause and re-focus attention. Simply search under the apps. There are always exciting new programs coming out!

Mindfulness may involve different aspects:

- Gaining distance from our internal thoughts, which seem like reality, to appreciate that they are simply our own thoughts and that they do not require us to get involved.
- Describing what is in front of us, which helps prevent us from worrying about things that happened in the past or that may happen in the future.
- Suspending judgment about whether something is good or bad, important or not as judgments are not reality and can increase our level of anxiety. Rather than judging what is happening, mindfulness encourages us to describe it.
- Taking yourself out of the center of worries and keeping in mind that some things are not about you and cannot be controlled by you.

From The worry cure: Seven steps to stop worry from stopping you, by Robert L. Leahy, PhD)

Mindfulness has increasingly made its way into classrooms. Teachers might introduce exercises such as ringing a bell and having students slowly raise their hands when they can no longer hear the sound, or having students eat a small piece of chocolate and notice the way the sugar wakes up their taste buds, or having students walk around the schoolyard slowly and silently while noticing every part of each step they take (*Harvard Magazine*, A Classroom in the Now, October 17, 2913). Such exercises, according to mindfulness practice, help promote self-awareness, which is critical in managing stress, especially in a world in which we are all faced with constant input and updates through technology and social media (ibid.). Kabat-Zinn reinforced the importance of instead of simply telling students to pay attention, showing them how to pay attention through experience. This, he maintained, is how students can learn to make better decisions in stressful situations rather than after the fact (ibid.). "Mindfulness is like a muscle, and without exercises it will lose its strength," he said. "Our world is so much about *doing* that the *being* gets lost" (ibid.). Also, according to mindfulschools.org, mindfulness brings about a whole range

of benefits, including ability to focus attention, emotional regulation, adaptability, sense of compassion, calming of the body, as well as promotion of resiliency.

Furthermore, research has found that mindfulness practice can help improve interoceptive awareness (Mahler, year, p. 69). By paying attention to the present internal body sensations, like breathing and muscle tension, mindfulness helps build interoceptive awareness. Neurological evidence for this has been found in those people he engaged in regular mindfulness meditation; they have both a thicker and more active insula—the part of the brain we discussed earlier that is activated during processing of our internal sensation and during tasks that elicit our emotions (Mahler, year, p. 69).

For more information, check out:
- www.mindfulschools.org/training, which offers online training
- www.mindfulnesseveryday.org
- or search for local courses in your city/town.

Cognitive Behavioral Therapy

In cognitive behavioral therapy (CBT), individuals learn to stop and challenge thoughts, attitudes, and beliefs that underlie emotional and behavioral responses and ultimately anxiety. CBT helps reduce anxiety by teaching people how to:

- Notice distortions in their thinking.
- See thoughts only as possible ideas about what is occurring instead of facts.
- Create distance from their thoughts to consider different possibilities

(http://www.camh.ca/en/hospital/health_information/a_z_mental_health_and_addiction_information/CBT/Pages/default.aspx).

At the beginning of therapy, the focus is mainly on highlighting factors that may be maintaining anxiety and/or depression, such as negative thinking patterns (e.g., thoughts, beliefs, assumptions, attitudes, worries) and behaviors (e.g., avoidance, withdrawal, excessive reassurance-seeking). Underlying this type of therapy is the idea that distorted patterns of thinking can lead to worsened experiences of negative emotions, physical symptoms, and unproductive behaviors (www.foresthillcbt.com). Changing the patterns of our thinking can lead to more positive experiences of positive emotions and behaviors and better physical health.

Executive Functions and Character Development

Throughout our day, we rely on our executive functions to successfully go to work or school, perform tasks independently, and relate well to others. These skills are directed by the frontal lobe in our brain. Examples of executive functions include (http://www.ldonline.org/article/29122/):

- *Inhibition:* The ability to stop one's own behaviour at an appropriate time, including one's actions and thoughts. (If you have trouble with this skill, you appear impulsive.)
  Example: Johnny is eyeing the cupcakes at the corner of the classroom his Mom has sent for his birthday that day to share with his class. He knows he has to wait until it is time to eat them together as a class.

- *Shift:* The ability to move freely from one situation to another as well as think flexibly to respond appropriately to a situation.
  Example: Wanda is really enjoying the discussion on pandas; she knows a lot about pandas as they are her favorite animal and has much information to share. All of a sudden, Ms. Sweet starts speaking about reptiles instead. Wanda feels a bit disappointed at first but then remembers some of the interesting facts she learned about reptiles on her last class visit to the zoo.

- *Emotional control:* The ability to modulate emotional responses by bringing rational thought to consider feelings.
  Example: Dario is upset that the other students keep brushing against him in the line-up as they wait to go the library that day. He doesn't think he can take it one more time. However, then he thinks to himself, "Maybe I should just try standing in the back of the line instead. Maybe I'm over-reacting a bit because I'm feeling quite tired, I didn't like the last class, and I am worried about tryouts after school today."

- *Initiation:* The ability to begin a talk or activity and independently generate ideas and responses or problem solve strategies.
  Example: Mr. LeBlanc has divided the class into small groups to present on one of the French books they have been studying that term. Maddy is worried that nobody is taking on the leader role in her group to decide who will play what character and what spin they will take on the story. "Never mind," she thinks to herself, "I guess I'm up to the challenge." She takes charge and assigns students to roles in the play.

- *Working memory:* The capacity to hold information in mind for the purpose of completing a task.

Example: Chris is trying to remember his new friend's email address during drama class period since he doesn't have paper to write the address down.

- *Planning/organization:* The ability to manage current and future-oriented task demands.
  Example: Tricia is busy planning who she wants to invite to her birthday party in two weeks while she rides home on her bike.

- *Organization of materials:* The ability to organize materials and space needed for work, play, and storage.
  Example: Mr. Smith is impressed with how well Ricardo is managing his desk space. It is neat and organized with all of his binders, notebooks, and pencils on one side and his fidget items on the other.

- Self-monitoring: The ability to monitory one's own performance and to measure it against some standard of what is needed or expected.
  Example: James realizes that everyone around him seems to be on the last page of the English test and there are only five minutes left in the period. "I better pick up the pace," he thinks to himself.

The ability to successfully self-regulate and reliably rely on executive functions can also greatly affect students' character development. It can help motivate them to make positive contributions to their school and community as well as think critically and creatively (http://www.tdsb.on.ca/elementaryschool/the-classroom/characterdevelopment.aspx).

A solid foundation and knowledge about your own skills, strengths, and challenges can have a positive effect on your ability to react when faced with stressors and enable you to use effective strategies when faced with challenges. When your body does not feel calm and organized and you are not regulated, you are coping. It is quite difficult to demonstrate the characteristics listed above when you are overwhelmed and coping in the fight/flight/fright/or shutdown mode. This will be discussed in more detail in Chapter 7.

By helping students in school learn more about their executive functions and promote their sense of self-awareness, we can help empower them and help them become as successful as possible at school; we accomplish this by helping them regulate their behavior and thinking. There is a growing awareness of this in our schools as talk about executive functions becomes increasingly popular. One great program was developed by educators Mara Berzins and Nicola Daykin through research and professional development of executive functions at Montcrest School in Toronto. This program introduces students to 10 key executive function skills through characters that represent each skill, such as Gracie Goal Getter and Suzie Shifter, or 10 executive function "superheroes." The program includes activities to practice, like the "blow off steam" routine when a teacher sees that a class is challenged by executive functions, as well as ready-made lesson plans, such as scenario role play to help develop critical thinking skills for possible scenarios that may happen at school. Berzins and Daykin suggested that the program is best used school-wide so that students learn a common language that is consistent in their different classes and grades. This also helps them continue to practice and develop their skills each year at school.

For more information, see: http://efs2therescue.ca

Other recommendations to promote the development of executive functions in the classroom include:
- Reduce sensory distractions in the classroom when possible.
- Promote routine and predictability, especially with visual schedules.
- "Emotional previewing" helps to warn a student that the next activity may be particular challenging and to think of strategies to get through successfully.
- Check off goals as they are met.
- Break goals into smaller components to help with a sense of accomplishment.
- Introduce calming/organizing strategies before a student starts to escalate.
- Model strategies and calming your body in front of students by verbalizing the process.

The ability to successfully self-regulate and reliably rely on your executive functions can also greatly affect students' character development. It can help motivate them to make positive contributions to their school and community as well as think critically and creatively (http://www.tdsb.on.ca/elementaryschool/theclassroom/characterdevelopment.aspx).

Examples of these character traits include:
- Respect
- Empathy
- Responsibility
- Cooperation
- Kindness
- Perseverance
- Fairness
- Teamwork
- Integrity
- Honesty

Without a solid foundation for your own skills, strengths, and challenges, how you react to many stressors, and ideas for strategies you can try when faced with challenges or when your body does not feel calm and organized, it would be quite difficult to demonstrate these characteristics. A person, instead, may be working in fight/flight/fright/or shutdown mode.

Chapter Seven

Moving Forward Together

Learning Objectives—
In this chapter, teachers and students will learn:

- About character development
- Ideas for self-regulation
- Ideas to encourage their character development in a fun and creative way

A review of sensory processing, regulation, interoception, executive functions and regulation programs are also included in this chapter.

Teachers play an integral and vital role in preparing our children for life. Their job has become increasing difficult. Classrooms contain children with various challenges. Some have individual education plans and others need support but do not have an individual education plan. We have children in our classrooms who have arrived from far away places that are learning English and who may be recovering from a traumatic exit from their homeland. In each classroom, many countries of the world are represented in the faces of the children and the teachers. There are many cultures, values, faiths, and ways of expression in each classroom. It seems an insurmountable task when we look at all of our differences. The only solution is to look at what we have in common. We are all human with a need to belong and feel like we are part of a group. We want to learn, grow and have the necessary skills to meet the demands of life when we become adults. We all have a nervous system that processes sensation and understanding that basic similarity can provide a common understanding of each other. Behaviours can be viewed through a lens of understanding and solutions are easier to find when judgements are suspended. Teachers need to be a 'jack of all trades' and their job is one of the most important jobs in our society.

Teacher assistants are often shared amongst classes and they do their best to support students who have a variety of needs. The job of teachers and teacher assistants is to move this diverse group through a curriculum to prepare them for the following year. That is a tall order! Teachers need to be armed with understanding, knowledge, creativity, enthusiasm and support from their administrators and from parents. As the teachers support the learning of the students, we support the teachers. It does take a village to raise a child!

When you drive past any school in Toronto, you will often see a character of the month on the sign in front of the school. The characters are:

- Respect
- Kindness
- Integrity
- Empathy
- Perseverance
- Honesty
- Responsibility
- Fairness
- Cooperation
- Teamwork

What a wonderful goal! Enabling students to develop these character traits sounds like a wonderful idea, but how do we do that? How do we develop character?

Character takes many years to develop. Research supports that self-regulation skills and emotional regulation skills, necessary for the development of character, continue to develop well into our early twenties. (Shankar Pg 33; ACT for Youth, 2002). Our character continues to develop throughout our life. Our successes and failures in meeting the demands of our environment help to make up our character. Our parents, family members, and teachers educate us on how to conduct ourselves. They provide the feedback we need, whether positive or negative, to help shape our character. There are no shortcuts to character development. It takes work, time, experience, honest feedback, and opportunities to try again.

The starting point in developing character is self-knowledge. Who is the person we would be proud to be? Who do we look up to? How do we want to interact with others? We have to know ourselves first. How do we work? What do we like/dislike? What environments do we succeed in? Which approaches work best in interacting with others? What activities are we best at?

The previous chapters of this book have provided many opportunities to investigate and learn the answers to these questions. This learning is vital to children in discovering who they are, how they work, and what they like. Armed with this knowledge, children can set goals for themselves and make a plan to achieve them. How do you plan your life when you don't know where you're going? How do you know where you're going if you don't know yourself?

Character traits enable us to be aware of others in our group and to watch out for them. Our brains are wired to be social and character enables the maintenance of these social bonds. We understand that we are part of a larger group and when one of us is successful, all of us are successful. Character enables us to invest in each other; to take the time to understand another's perspective, to assume responsibility for our actions, and demonstrate respect and kindness for others. Character enables us to stick with a difficult task until it's complete—even if it's difficult. Character helps us to work on teams and be responsible to our fellow teammates. It supports honesty and integrity so that people in our groups can depend on us to do the things we say we will do. When we develop character, we develop a sense of who we are. We can predict how we will act in different situations, and develop a confidence in ourselves and an identity. These skills definitely prepare children for life in a society and help build strong citizens that can keep our society strong and unified. Character development is an excellent investment!

The bell rang for recess. Kelvin was trying to clean up his workstation and kept dropping papers on the floor. The faster he tried to clean up, the slower he got! Ella was putting on her coat and getting her skipping rope for recess when she saw Kelvin struggling. She really wanted to get outside to skip but she stopped, put her skipping rope down, and helped Kelvin pick up his papers.

Ella missed two minutes of recess, but she and Kelvin got to enjoy most of recess. Ella was aware of herself and her friend. She demonstrated kindness in her actions, one of the character traits on the Toronto Board of Education character list.

Review of Sensory Processing

In this curriculum, we have learned that our sensory systems give us information about ourselves, and our environments. Sensory processing is working from the very beginning, feeding our nervous systems with information, even before we are born! With repeated exposure to sensation, the connections between the neurons become insulated and we become more efficient at processing sensations and executing responses. We learn about what sensations we enjoy. We also learn that some sensations can be difficult for us to process, so we can avoid those sensations. As we grow, we learn about our body and our environment and the world becomes a more predictable place. Efficient sensory processing also enables us to subconsciously process sensation that is unchanging so that we can pay attention to new sensation in our environment. In the above example, Ella was able to process her tactile, vestibular, proprioceptive, auditory, and visual information efficiently. She was also able to execute her motor plan of putting on her coat automatically without conscious attention. Because of her efficiency, she was able to notice Kelvin's difficulty and assist him. Her sensory processing provided information about what was happening and her character enabled her to make the decision to help.

Review of Regulation

Efficient sensory processing can contribute to efficient regulation skills. When we understand which sensations are processed more efficiently, we can seek them out to help maintain our nervous system in a regulated state. On the other hand, when we know which sensations are challenging to process, we can prepare for events that contain the more challenging sensations and use strategies to manage the sensations so that we can stay in a regulated state.

We also learn to regulate our nervous systems by learning regulating behaviours from others. Our first relationships are with our parents. We bond with our parents and learn that when we are upset, we are comforted. When we are hungry, we are fed. Our parents co-regulate with us to help us grow and learn how to maintain our own calm alert state. Before we are able to self-regulate, we learn to co-regulate, match or adjust our level of energy, alertness, and emotion to coordinate with those around us. Adults teach and model self-regulation skills for children so they can learn how to self-regulate. Parents and teachers can be excellent role models of self-regulation. Teachers can facilitate co-regulation activities in the classroom setting to help their students stay calm and focused on the lesson. An example of a self-regulation activity could be 4 square breathing where teachers and students slowly breathe in and out as the teacher moves their hand along each side of the square.

Many of the techniques we use to calm ourselves and each other are sensory techniques. These techniques can include rocking, singing, hugging, smelling a familiar scent, petting a family pet, or sharing a meal. We can also decrease the sensory input to enable us to self-regulate and can go into a dark, quiet room when we are overwhelmed.

When we are upset or overwhelmed, we may feel scared or frustrated. Our parents comfort us, and we can feel calm, supported and happy again. We learn that emotions are often attached to sensory experiences. The experiences of sensations and emotions become our first memories. We reference our memories throughout our lifetime. They contribute to our understanding of who we are.

Review of Interoception

The interoception system is the sensory system that ties everything together: sensation, emotion, and executive functions. As our nervous system matures, we use our interoception system to automatically scan our body and our emotional state. When we learn to interpret interoception, we know the state of our nervous system and the emotion we are feeling. When we recognize our state, we can choose a strategy to maintain it or change it to return to the 'just right' state; the state of regulation. It is in the 'just right' state that sensory processing, emotional processing, and cognitive processing all work together most efficiently. This is the state of learning. It is in this state that we learn about ourselves.

Feelings of competence develop when we know ourselves and what we can do. When we feel competent in our skills, we can develop confidence and take the risks necessary for learning.

When we develop a sense of who we are, we are able to learn that we also belong to our family, our classroom, our faith, and our society. We develop our character, which guides our interactions with the people in our life.

The Sensory Detective Curriculum was written to share information and strategies to encourage the understanding of the underlying neurology of regulation from a sensory perspective. Regulation is possible only when our nervous system is in a calm and alert state. Sensory processing is one of the tools that we can use to support the development of regulation. The development of our character is only possible when the nervous system is regulated.

Stuart Shanker is one of Canada's leading experts on self-regulation. He recognizes that teachers play a very important role in helping students develop self-regulation. (Stuart Shankar, pg. 93). Self-regulation enables many skills according to Dr. Shankar. The ability to self-regulate enables us to recognize which emotions are ours and which belong to another person. The ability to deal with stressors in other dimensions of self- regulation are better in students who can self-regulate.

Some examples:

- *An example of biological regulation:* Amilee feels hungry and wants to go get her snack in her knapsack. She looks at the clock and sees that there are only five minutes remaining until lunch. She decides she can wait.

- *An example of emotional regulation:* Aberdeen says hello to her friend Jayden and Jayden ignores her. Aberdeen felt surprised by Jayden's lack of response. Then she remembered that Jayden had an ear infection and probably didn't hear her. She caught up with Jayden and said hello again in Jayden's field of vision. Jayden smiled and said "Hi girl!"

- *An example of cognitive regulation:* Mackenzie looked down at his exam. He blanked at question one. "Keep calm", he thought, "what was my clue again? Oh yeah! This answer rhymes with motion... ocean!" He wrote the answer on the exam.

- *An example of social regulation:* Jackson saw his friends at the school fair and began to introduce them to his parents but he could not remember their names. He began by telling a little story about how he and his friends helped the teacher bring the ice down from the staff room and then ... pop! ... the names were available to him. "Mom and dad, I'd like to introduce you to Sarah and Cameron, my best friends in school!"

In each of these examples, the regulated state of the student enabled executive functions to be used. Executive functions enable us to fine tune and modify behaviour and are dependent on efficient sensory processing and regulation and are necessary for the development of character.

The ability to self-regulate and recognize our own emotions and the emotions of others helps us develop empathy according to Dr. Shankar, and empathy enables us to understand others and can decrease the incidence of bullying.

The ability of a student to regulate his or her own feelings and emotions is a very important life skill. Strong emotions can be disregulating. The negative emotions experienced when a student failed a test can be equally disregulating as the praise another student received from the teacher. Processing strong emotions requires energy. Regulating our emotions is an energy saver—leaving more energy for learning and interacting at school. Social and emotional learning are just as important as teaching reading and writing in school according to Dr. Shankar.

Individuals with self-regulation skills can react to unexpected sensory events throughout their day such as: a light unexpected touch, a forgotten book, or the sound of a fire alarm, but they are able to recover and keep their nervous system in the 'just right' state. Individuals who are more defensive to sensory input react to those same events but are unable to recover and become more disregulated as the day goes on. Sensory events can 'add up' and create explosive behaviour that may be difficult to predict. Some children keep all their defensive responses inside and explode when they arrive home. Parents and teachers who communicate daily can support children with a sensitive nervous system much better.

Oliver's day began with a fire drill that he did not expect. The shrill sound startled him and he ran from the class. Later that day, he was still disregulated and pulled his friend's hair. He did not recover from the fire alarm and continued to be disregulated throughout the day.

Review of Executive Functions

We rely on our executive functions to successfully go to work and/or school, perform tasks independently, and relate well to others. Executive functions include: inhibition, shift, emotional control, initiation, working memory, planning, organizing materials, and self-monitoring. Efficient sensory processing and regulation are necessary supports to the development and use of executive functions and executive functions are the support to the development of character.

The ability to successfully self-regulate and reliably rely on executive functions can also greatly affect students' character development. It can help motivate them to make positive contributions to their school and community as well as think critically and creatively (www.tdsb.on.ca/elementaryschool/theclassroom/characterdevelopment.aspx).

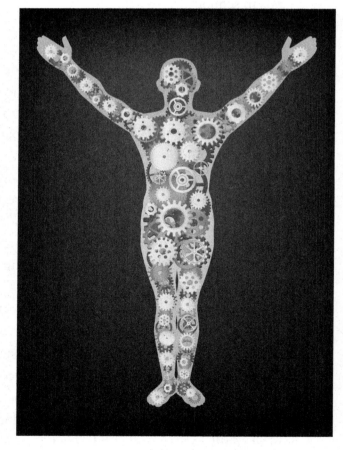

In our practice, we have had the opportunity to visit many schools and see first hand how students with differences in their learning are supported. It is easy to take a linear view and look at the school's ability or their lack of ability to support their students. We need to step back at look at the support of students from a wider angle. Are the teachers supported by the principal, is the principal supported by the board, are the parents supported by the school, is the school supported by the parents, and are students supportive of other students? What we are talking about is a culture of acceptance and learning.

As professionals who support students who learn differently, we often work in isolation. We assess our own areas of a student's performance. Students need us to cross our boundaries and see them as a whole person. We need to put our heads together, so we can gain a perspective of the "entire" person and incorporate strategies for the student that are functional and customized to increase school success. We also have to share our knowledge with the student, the parents, the school and each other.

One of the most important needs in children is to belong. In one school it was suggested that children in a very active autism classroom be kept inside during recess in case they ran out of the schoolyard. The teachers and principals felt strongly that the children in this class should be out enjoying the playground like everyone else. They put neon orange vests on each student so that they could be easily seen and positioned the recess monitors near the exits to the playground to discourage leaving the area. The children were overjoyed at the ability to play in the playground. They did not attempt to leave; they were too busy having fun! Their classroom teacher noticed increased regulation of behaviour after recess. Was it the sensations of running, climbing and playing that contributed to the increase in behavioural regulation or was it the feeling of belonging? Probably all!

Elan was so excited to be in the cafeteria with his friends during lunch, he was shouting and singing. Leah knew that Elan was excited and that he tended to use his outdoor voice when he was excited so she sat down beside him and quietly asked him questions about dinosaurs. Elan was able to make his voice quiet as he described the terrible teeth of tyrannosaurus rex. Leah was able to model a regulated voice volume and Elan was able to co-regulate with Leah.

Kindness and empathy can empower students with self-awareness and strategies to deal with frustration. It helps students understand each other better and choose strategies that support each other.

Noah wanted Aubrey's baseball during lunch recess, but Aubrey wanted to play catch with Simon. Noah became frustrated and started to push Aubrey. Aubrey remembered other strategies that he could use to dissipate the situation. Instead of pushing Noah back, Aubrey responded with kindness and said, 'I think it's cool that you like my baseball. I'm using it now, but you can use it when I'm done." Aubrey gave Noah a compliment and then promised him his baseball when he was finished playing. Noah felt heard and acknowledged and was able to calm down.

Aubrey understood Noah's frustration through his empathy for Noah. This enabled him to choose a kind response, which helped Noah regain his regulated state.

Review of Regulation Programs

There are many ways that we can work on incorporating self-regulation into the curriculum in schools. There are some wonderful programs to explore:

- *The Alert Program* by Sherry Shellenberger and Mary Sue Williams
  This program uses the analogy that our body runs like a car engine, either "too high", "too low", or in the "just right" speed to help teach self-regulation to students. Top-down approaches are used,

teaching cognitive and language strategies to become aware of the body's state. Bottom-up approaches are also used by introducing various sensory strategies to help change engine speed. They aim to empower individuals to become more aware of their body states and be able to eventually problem-solve independently which sensory strategies they can use to self-regulate.

- *The Incredible 5 Point Scale* by Kari Dunn Buron
  This program was designed to help students with anxiety cope with their stress by systematically organizing social and emotional information. Students sort cards that describe varying situations that they may find stressful into different coloured pockets. The pockets are labeled from 1 to 5 to indicate how stressed they think they would feel in that situation. This program offers an anxiety scale, which makes the process of escalation and de-escalation visual, a worry book, and a check in system.

- *The Zones of Regulation* by Leah Kuypers
  This program is a top-down approach and uses cognitive and language strategies to teach self-regulation. Students learn to self-regulate by categorizing the ways they feel into four zones (represented by traffic signs). The program aims to teach students to become more aware of the state of their nervous system and emotions, become better at controlling their emotions and impulses, problem-solve their sensory needs, and help students solve conflicts. This program uses a social thinking curriculum.

- *Stop Now and Plan* by The Child Development Institute in Toronto
  The Stop Now and Plan (SNAP) program was created as a cognitive behavioural strategy and helps teach children to stop before carrying out their automatic response so that they can try to think of a more appropriate way of reacting. The program includes behaviours such as, taking a deep breath or counting to 10. It also includes a cognitive component, such as, thinking of calming thoughts or coping statements such as, "This is hard, but I can do it". It also involves developing a plan for the next steps to take.

Building self-regulation skills and building a community where everyone belongs are keys to successful students. When students feel like they belong they can take responsibility for their space.

Eitan walked through the hallway and saw a discarded water bottle. "That doesn't belong here", he thought, "Someone could slip on it." He picked it up and put it in the recycling container.

Eitan felt a sense of responsibility as he felt this school was his school and he was proud of it. He wanted to take care of it.

Executive Function 2 the Rescue

There is a growing awareness about executive functions in our schools and recognition of their importance throughout a student's academic career. Educators Mara Berzins and Nicola Daykin, at the Moncrest School in Toronto, developed a wonderful program to build executive function skills in students called Executive Functions 2 the Rescue. This program introduces students to 10 key executive function skills through characters that represent each skill i.e., Gracie Goal Getter and Suzie Shifter, or 10 EF "superheroes." The program also includes activities to practice, like their "blow off steam" routine. This program strives to develop critical thinking skills through possible scenarios that could happen at school. Berzins and Daykin see the program best used school-wide so that students learn a common language that is consistent among their different classes and grades. This also helps them continue to practice and develop their skills each year at school.

For more information, go to: http://efs2therescue.ca

General ideas we can incorporate in schools to help build students' overall self-regulation and build a culture of acceptance, belonging and community:

- "Check-in" periodically during class to see how students are doing and feeling.
- In circle time or at the end of the day, have students give the person to their left a compliment.
- At the end of the day, have students reflect on what was their high point of the day or the low point of their day? What were they most proud of?
- Teachers can nominate five "everyday heroes" as often as they like to help students develop both self-awareness and well as the awareness of actions of other students.
- Teachers can create an award wall in the class to highlight students' accomplishments.
- At home, parents can help develop an award wall in front of the spot where their child completes their homework as motivation.
- At the end of the day, students can go around and say something nice about someone in class (or you can have them pick out of a hat). They can write these compliments down and you can create a positivity wall in you class.
- You can help students build a sense of community by pairing them up for different tasks that a student may need help in. Examples could include:
  - Recess angels to help problem-solve challenges that arise during recess
  - Peer helpers
  - Reading buddies with a student from a younger grade

Teaching regulation and executive functions into our classrooms enable us to help students:

- Increase their self-awareness
- Advocate for what they need
- Increase understanding of the needs of their friends
- Advocate for friends

Character Development from a Sensory Perspective

In this final section of the book, we have listed strategies to build the character traits from a sensory, physical, arts, classroom space, community space and social point of view. There are wonderful ideas from many disciplines listed here (even from the experiences of camp!) but these ideas are by no means exhaustive; they are a starting point. Be sure to be creative! Discussion following the activities can enrich the children's learning. Provide opportunities for reflection and encourage the students to transfer their learning to their day-to-day activities. Parent information sheets can be provided to keep parents up-to-date on what is happening in the classroom. Discussions can continue at home and learning can be further enhanced. Share and discuss stories already in the curriculum and stories from personal experience to broaden understanding.

1. Respect

- we can respect that students with SPD are doing their best everyday
- even though their behaviour can seem difficult, wilful or manipulative, we can respect the immense effort students with SPD uses to be in school
- we can use sensory supports without calling too much attention to the student or singling them out
- we can give students with SPD choices and respect their choice
- we can respect that the frustration and overwhelmed state of students may be expressed through language, through physiology or through behaviour
- respect the need for movement, stretching and breathing; it can be built right into the daily schedule and will benefit all students
- respect recess; don't use it as a punishment. Recess is non-negotiable
- respect the need for personal space, breaks and modifications to the environment, approach and activities

Physical activities that support understanding and the practice of Respect:

- yoga—respect the limits of your body and what feels good to you
- human obstacle course—ask students to line up in different positions and have them move through the obstacle course without touching others and to remember to respect personal space
- musical chairs—respect the music's direction
- Twister
- hopscotch—respect where the bean bag lands
- Mother May I?—respect the answer

Arts

- each student makes a life size outline of themselves and on the torso, they list five things they like about themselves. Then each student lists a characteristic they admire about that person on each outline. Read them out loud.
- Drama scenes (that can be created from the imagination or from actual events in your class)—discuss how the voice volume, choice of words and body language communicated respect and why.
  Classroom Space
- Check in to see that your items are not spilling onto your friend's desk or cubby. If they are, clean them up.
- Ensure books are returned in the right place, scissors are returned blades down, pencils are returned sharpened, etc.

Community Space

- park/schoolyard clean up
- reduce, reuse, and recycle
- care for nature around your school

Social

- inclusion days—make them as fun as possible—the message is that everyone is respected and everyone belongs (pyjama day, younger brother day, seven-year-old day, sparkly belt day, etc.)
- create opportunities in the classroom to honor parents and grandparents

2. Empathy

- the child with SPD cannot be flexible, so we need to be flexible
- we can understand that a student with SPD cannot modulate and modify their responses and they are not consistent in their responses
- we can acknowledge that students with SPD use so much effort, internal resources, strength and coping skills and yet they continue to try

- we can remember that sometimes tasks that we find easy can seem insurmountable to other students
- we can delay our activities to help out a fellow student with a difficulty
- we can offer support to a student who may have had a difficult time; say hi tomorrow morning and press the re-start button
- we can acknowledge the huge effort by teachers to create sensory learning environments sometimes with little space or resources
- we can appreciate how hard parents are working to care for their children and coordinate efforts with the school

Physical activities that support understanding and the practice of empathy:
- relay races
- three-legged race
- two student carry with square grip (each child has the opportunity to be carried and to carry another student)
- charades—students predict what the actor is experiencing

Arts
- look at art and guess what the artist was feeling when the picture was created
- look at dancing and guess what the dancer is expressing
- mirroring exercise—one student acts out a movement with facial expressions and another mirrors the actions
- creating cards/banners to celebrate or provide good wishes to students/staff

Classroom Space
- classroom pet to care for
- connect with another classroom in another country/inner city/or various communities to share experiences and resources

Community Space
- raise money for a food bank
- visit a retirement home
- visit an animal shelter

Social
- connect with a student you don't know well and get to know them
- recall a situation where you needed someone to understand your perspective

3. Responsibility

- we have a responsibility to update the sensory curriculum regularly to accommodate developmental changes, changing interests and age
- we have a responsibility to teach and model organization skills which are essential for school, work, and life
- we have a responsibility to model and teach self-regulation skills
- we have a responsibility to teach executive function skills (problem solving, planning, assessing, foreseeing consequences of behaviour, inhibition of responses, controlling impulses, flexible thinking, organization, learning from experience and feelings, time management)
- we have a responsibility to include everyone
- we have a responsibility to take care of ourselves and each other
- we are responsible to have sensory opportunities built right into classroom duties (movement for delivery, heavy work in carrying books, smells through cooking class, tactile needs through art)
- participation in duties can create a sense of responsibility and a sense of being needed
- we have the responsibility to communicate with our team in order for consistency in supporting the student with SPD

Physical activities that support understanding and the practice of responsibility:
- build a human pyramid
- relay race
- team sports

Arts
- Create a vision for yourself such as a life map, which lists where you are and where you want to go. Have it reflect your interests, goals, and what's important to you
- group art project
- play
- dance

Classroom Space
- duties for each member of the class
- caring for a classroom pet
- caring for plants/garden
- create a 'my talent jar' that includes your talents that can make your classroom and school better

Community Space
- food drives
- park clean up
- reduce, reuse, and recycle

Social
- buddy system in the classroom where you check in everyday to see how your buddy is doing
- recess buddies
- reading/math/any subject buddies

4. Cooperation

- we can work with the student to plan strategies for success in regulation, school function and executive functions
- we can work with parents to build a consistent approach for students with SPD
- we can build cooperation with the give and take games and participation in regulation programs
- we can build cooperation by sharing information so that the student knows what is coming up
- we can build cooperation by listening to each other and sharing humour

Physical activities that support understanding and the practice of cooperation:
- three-legged race
- over and under relay game
- egg and spoon race
- human pyramid
- broken telephone
- team sports

Arts
- group art project (e.g., Diorama of the school)
- group dance
- group drama presentation
- building a snow fort
- tea ceremony

Classroom Space
- perform duties/chores in groups of two or more students
- pot luck lunch
- pot luck picnic
- cooking activities

Community Space
- fundraising (bake sales) to support a school team, drama club, band, and choir or art club
- presentations to community schools, retirement homes, daycares
- participation in a community garden or beautification project

Social
- classroom helps
- hall monitors
- recess buddies
- reading any subject with buddies
- write a cooperative letter or story

5. Kindness

- we can recognize the effort that goes into trying, noticing and supporting the efforts of others
- we can delay our own gratification to make sure that everyone moves forward
- we can modify our classroom to ensure that sensory needs can be met
- we can modify our approach to match each other's sensory needs
- we can modify schoolwork (allow a student to complete work in parts, work standing up, take tests orally, give extra time)
- we can slow down our interaction with each other to accommodate sensory processing delays, anxiety, and organization difficulties
- we can provide positive feedback to each other
- we can celebrate each other's successes
- we can make sure that everyone feels included, important and part of the group

Physical activities that support understanding and the practice of kindness:
- Mother May I?
- clapping games

- skipping games
- relays
- three-legged race
- folk dances
- native dances

Arts

- create a kindness catcher role—a student who sees kindness in the classroom and writes/draws it on the board
- create art to recognize the kindness in ourselves and others
- which plays/movies show kindness?

Classroom space

- caring for a class pet
- caring for a garden
- creating a kindness jar (acts of kindness are placed within and read at the end of the week)
- maintaining a bird feeder/water bath

Community space

- preparing a basket of art/baked goods for a shelter/clothing drive
- preparing a play/dance for a retirement home
- making a community space cleaner

Social

- compliment game which recognizes acts of kindness in one another
- awards ceremony at the end of the week that recognizes students/teachers/parents who have been kind

6. Perseverance

- SPD causes function to be inconsistent—keep trying, keep supporting, keep teaching
- provide regular sensory breaks to regain the calm and alert state in the nervous system to prevent shutting down, meltdowns, running away, over-activity, anxiety, and inattention
- don't give up in your efforts to interact and support students with SPD; be creative in your strategies until you are successful

- encourage students to learn from the natural consequences of their actions and understand that mistakes are a natural part of learning

Physical activities that support understanding and the practice of perseverance:
- long distance running
- yoga—holding postures
- learning how to breathe
- spoon and water relay—filling a bowl across the classroom one spoonful at a time

Arts
- long term arts project (knitting, macramé, embroidery, woodworking, sculpture, clay)
- dance that takes many weeks to learn
- play that takes many weeks of practice

Classroom space
- continuing to tidy (even though it just gets messy again)
- pen pals where snail mail is used
- putting away library books in the correct place
- finishing your work—no giving up! Breaks are ok

Community space
- planting a garden
- teaching younger children recess games

Social
- mirroring rhythms that are made by one member of the group
- classroom buddies—consistently checking in to see if they are ok or need anything

7. Fairness

- students with SPD have many strengths and interests, find out what they are, label them and use them
- give students with SPD opportunities to share their strengths—let them teach the unit on dinosaurs
- set up the classroom environment with sensory needs in mind by modifying the environment to match the sensory needs of the teacher and student (minimize clutter and noise, have a quiet place, give space)

- provide students with SPD choices and opportunities to enjoy student life just like every other student
- we all learn in different ways and have different strengths
- students with SPD may find group work challenging, it may be fair to have them do an independent project or a project with one friend
- a student with SPD may need to use a computer or draw an assignment if writing is challenging
- make accommodations available to the whole class so that the student with SPD doesn't feel different or not able to do the task
- offer learning in the sensory modality that is easiest to process for this student
- modify tasks whenever necessary to build successful experiences
- give a student with dyspraxia lots of time to organize a response

Physical activities that support understanding and the practice of fairness:
- European handball—everyone must touch the ball before it goes to the net
- basketball hoops—everyone gets a shot—some from the floor and some from the ladder
- take turns during folk dancing
- skipping

Arts
- a banner or art project that everyone contributes to
- folk dancing
- poetry reading where everyone has a line to read

Classroom space
- rotating duty roster for classroom duties
- individualized movement breaks on top of classroom movement breaks if necessary
- show and tell

Community space
- posters to remind dog walkers to clean up after their dog
- signs reminding drivers where to park and to drive slowly to allow time for children to cross the road

Social
- giving everyone a chance to perform different duties in the classroom
- encouraging students to vocalize what they need to be successful
- buddy system—check in with your class buddy to see if they are ok and if they need anything

8. Teamwork

- identify sensory strengths and challenges and share it with the team (sensory lifestyle)
- integrate sensory strengths into daily activities with the goal of consistency across settings
- everyone can support in different ways
- have someone at the school who has a relationship with the student whom the student can go to see on challenging days. This person can be the liaison between the home and school and can monitor progress of the student
- problem-solve together to discover the underlying reasons for behaviours and strategies to try
- recognition that we are on the same team and everyone belongs
- when we move forward together, no one gets left behind

Physical activities that support understanding and the practice of teamwork:
- bridge over lava—everyone puts their shoes along the centre line of the gym and each class member must walk on the shoes to cross over the lava
- human pyramid
- any team sport
- dance club

Arts
- collaborative art project
- band producing a concert
- drama club producing a play
- choir producing a concert

Classroom space
- group work
- recognition of classroom helpers in the progress of the whole class
- cooking activities

Community space
- park clean up
- teamwork to prepare for a school fair
- fundraising for a community event (car wash, bake sale, dog grooming, make up studio)
- going for a Guinness World Record

Social
- buddy system
- problem-solving around a problem in the classroom
- supporting someone who is having difficulty in the classroom

9. Integrity

- educate the other students and staff members about SPD
- practice and model regulation strategies to regain the calm and alert state
- model what you teach and practice what you preach
- model empathy and other character traits so that others can learn from you
- model executive function skills so that others can learn from you
- interact with students at their level

Physical activities that support understanding and the practice of integrity:
- circle dance—there is an inside circle which goes clockwise and an outside circle that goes counter clockwise. The circles stop when the music stops and direction changes when the music starts again.
- North, South, East, West—every gym wall has a direction and when the direction is called out, children touch that wall

Arts
- watching a play and discussing the integrity of the characters
- draw/write about a time when you have exhibited integrity

Classroom space
- duties are performed to the expectations of the class
- items are returned to their correct place
- schedules warn of any changes to the day

Community space
- ensuring students behave in a way that best represents the school when they are on an outing
- schoolyard clean up—display a tidy space that students can be proud of

Social
- What would you do if ...?—situations are posed to students to see if they can predict what they would do

10. Honesty

- acknowledge our limitations in supporting a student with SPD
- we all need breaks and rest at times—model a choice to take a break
- some days we are not up for the task of supporting another student and that's ok, we can find someone else to step in
- if something is not working, acknowledge it and create a new strategy to try

Physical activities that support understanding and the practice of honesty:
- doggie doggie, who has your bone? Who has your iPad?—practice reading faces for honesty
- Mother May I
- What time is it Mr. Wolf?
- hide and seek—staying in the same spot; not changing
- dodge ball—acknowledging that you were hit
- tag—acknowledging that you were touched
- acknowledging your own needs for help, rest, etc

Arts
- public speaking—everyone gets a turn
- art—contributing your own work

Classroom space
- returning items belonging to others
- owning up to mistakes and broken items
- marking your own test

Community space
- owning up to community partners about mistakes

Social
- acknowledging mistakes and apologizing
- providing honest and positive feedback to friends

It definitely takes a village to raise a child (African proverb). Caring for each other, caring for ourselves, and making sure everyone feels included encompasses all of the character traits and ensures that everyone has the opportunity to learn.

Thank you for having fun and learning with *The Sensory Detective Curriculum*. We hope that you have enjoyed learning about sensory processing, the neurology of sensory processing and the assessment of sensory processing. We had fun in Chapter 4 discovering our own sensory preferences and challenges. Chapters 5 and 6 were full of strategies and ideas. We learned how to pull it all together in Chapter 7.

A society can only move forward at the speed of its most vulnerable individuals. Take care of each other!

Resources to Explore:

Second Step: a program for students from preschool to Grade 8 to help develop social-emotional skills, including empathy, as well as focuses on self-regulation. www.cfchildren.org/second-step/early-learning

Munoz, L.C., Qualter, P., Padgett, G. (2011). Empathy and bullying: Exploring the influence of callous-unemotional traits. *Child Psychiatry and Human Development*, 42, pp. 183–196.

Mahler, K. (2016). *Interoception—the eighth sensory system: Practical solutions for improving self-regulation, self-awareness and social understanding in individuals with Autism Spectrum and related disorders*. Lenaxa.

About the Authors

Paula Aquilla is a mom of two amazing girls. She, her husband, and daughters live in Toronto, Canada. Paula is an occupational therapist and an osteopathic manual practitioner. She is the director of Aquilla Occupational Therapy Services in Toronto. Paula is published in the field and has enjoyed sharing information about sensory processing through courses and workshops internationally. Paula brings warmth, fun, and creativity to her work with children and their families.

Alexi Edelstein is a new mom to a wonderful baby boy. She, her husband and son live in Toronto, Canada. Alexi is an occupational therapist and currently works at Aquilla Occupational Therapy Services with a particular interest in sensory processing. Alexi brings her passion and creativity to her work with families.

Paula Riczker lives in Toronto, Canada with her husband and three school-aged children. She is an occupational therapist who brings energy and fun to Aquilla Occupational Therapy Services.

Other Books by Paula Aquilla

Coming Soon!

Teach your children and students how our bodies process the environment. Whimsical illustrations are fun to color and easy to explore.

Color My Senses

The Sensory Detective Coloring Book

...ula Aquilla, BSc, OT

Building Bridges

Through Sensory Integration

Third Edition

Therapy for Children with Autism and Other Pervasive Developmental Disorders

Ellen Yack, BSc, MEd, OT & Paula Aquilla, BSc, OT & Shirley Sutton, BSc, OT

Foreword by Carol Kranowitz, MA

SMART BOOK AWARD WINNER

The classic therapy guide has been expanded for its third edition. Featuring all-new content, this book can be used for students of all ages.

CPSIA information can be obtained at www.ICGtesting.com
Printed in the USA
BVOW09s1740220716

456195BV00004B/7/P